TECHNICAL ANALYSIS OF GAPS

TECHNICAL ANALYSIS OF GAPS

IDENTIFYING PROFITABLE GAPS FOR TRADING

JULIE R. DAHLQUIST
RICHARD J. BAUER, JR.

Vice President, Publisher: Tim Moore
Associate Publisher and Director of Marketing: Amy Neidlinger
Executive Editor: Jim Boyd
Editorial Assistant: Pamela Boland
Operations Specialist: Jodi Kemper
Assistant Marketing Manager: Megan Graue
Cover Designer: Alan Clements
Managing Editor: Kristy Hart
Senior Project Editor: Lori Lyons
Copy Editor: Apostrophe Editing Services
Proofreader: Kathy Ruiz
Indexer: Lisa Stumpf
Compositor: Nonie Ratcliff
Manufacturing Buyer: Dan Uhrig

© 2012 by Julie R. Dahlquist / Richard J. Bauer, Jr.
Pearson Education, Inc.
Publishing as FT Press
Upper Saddle River, New Jersey 07458

FT Press offers excellent discounts on this book when ordered in quantity for bulk
purchases or special sales. For more information, please contact U.S. Corporate and
Government Sales, 1-800-382-3419, corpsales@pearsontechgroup.com. For sales outside the U.S., please contact International Sales at international@pearson.com.

Stock charts created with TradeStation. ©TradeStation Technologies, Inc. All rights
reserved.

Company and product names mentioned herein are the trademarks or registered
trademarks of their respective owners.

Printed in the United States of America

First Printing June 2012

ISBN-10: 0-13-290043-2
ISBN-13: 978-0-13-290043-0

Pearson Education LTD.
Pearson Education Australia PTY, Limited.
Pearson Education Singapore, Pte. Ltd.
Pearson Education Asia, Ltd.
Pearson Education Canada, Ltd.
Pearson Educación de Mexico, S.A. de C.V.
Pearson Education—Japan
Pearson Education Malaysia, Pte. Ltd.

Library of Congress Cataloging-in-Publication Data
Dahlquist, Julie R., 1962-
  Technical analysis of gaps : identifying profitable gaps for trading / Julie R.
Dahlquist, Richard J. Bauer, Jr.
    p. cm.
  ISBN 978-0-13-290043-0 (hbk. : alk. paper)
  1. Stocks—Charts, diagrams, etc. 2. Technical analysis (Investment analysis) I.
Bauer, Richard J., 1950- II. Title.
  HG4638.D34 2012
  332.63'2042—dc23
                                        2012010828

To Katherine and Sepp

Contents

Acknowledgments

We first started looking at gaps because they provide useful illustrations when teaching our students how to read stock charts. Students hear a news report that their favorite company just reported earnings, that a company is being sued, or that a well-known company, such as Apple, is launching a new product and ask how these events will affect the price of the stock of the company. These news events often trigger sizeable price moves, frequently on a gap. We can introduce the concept of a gap easily and quickly and then use the conversation as a jumping-off point for broader discussion of the tools of technical analysis.

Gaps repeatedly come up during small talk when people find out that we have a background in technical analysis. Even individuals who know little about the stock market seem to have heard the adage "the gap is always filled." The two technical analysis terms that people seem to latch on to are "head and shoulders" and "gaps." After engaging in a number of these conversations, we thought it would be interesting to pursue this topic a bit more. Gaps seem to have captured the attention of the earliest technical analysts, but we found surprisingly little systematic study of gaps. Much of the recent work in the area of technical analysis has been based on complex mathematical models. We thought it would be a fun and interesting endeavor to investigate one of the simple, basic ideas of technical analysis in more depth. Thus, a couple of years ago we began our inquiry.

In the beginning, we thought we would engage in a simple study that would provide some interesting stories regarding gaps to use in our classrooms. As we started looking at gaps, our appreciation for their use as a tool of technical analysis grew and our inquiry grew. In May 2011, we were honored as recipients of the Market Technicians Association's Charles H. Dow Award in Technical Analysis for our paper, "Analyzing Gaps for Profitable Trading Strategies." We realized that in our paper we had only been able to scratch the surface of gaps. Our editor, Jim Boyd, suggested we continue our investigation in the form of a book—the result of which you are holding in your hands.

We are indebted to a number of people who helped us learn more about gaps and who helped put this knowledge together in the form of this book. First, we are indebted to Charlie Kirkpatrick for all the support and assistance he has given us in learning about technical analysis over the years. His knowledge and patience are endless. Ellie Kirkpatrick, Charlie's wife, is the greatest cheerleader anyone could have in their corner. She continues to motivate and inspire us. We thank both Charlie and Ellie for the endless list of things that they have done for us and our children.

We would like to thank Fred Meissner and Hank Pruden for their support and encouragement. They are both stellar examples of the friendliness and warmth exhibited by many in the technical analysis community. They, too, have been especially kind to our children. Thanks to all those who work in the MTA office, especially Tom Silveri, Tim Licitra, and Shane Skwarek. This project has benefited from conversations with members of the MTA through electronic discussion groups, webinars, and meetings across the world—from Houston to

Prague. A special thanks to Robert Colby and Ralph Acampora for answering questions along the way. Thanks, also, to Norgate Investor Services for granting us permission to publish our results, which were based on their stock price data marketed as Premium Data.

We are grateful to the Pearson staff, especially executive editor Jim Boyd, managing editor Kristy Hart, and senior project editor Lori Lyons for their hard work and dedication in bringing this project to fruition.

We have dedicated this book to our children, Katherine and Sepp. They challenge, inspire, and entertain us in innumerable ways. It is bittersweet watching our children grow up. We miss their younger versions, but our relationship with them both deepens and becomes more meaningful and special with each passing year. We feel richly blessed with the honor of being their parents.

—Julie and Richard

Being able to undertake a project like this requires the encouragement and support of family, teachers, friends, and colleagues over a number of years. Thanks to my mom for encouraging me to pursue studies in economics and finance, although she claims not to understand anything about it herself. Thanks to my sisters, Carrie and Katie, for being there to laugh about old family stories whenever I need a break from work. Good luck to my nephew, John, as he embarks upon his college career!

—Julie

I want to thank family members for their support. I thank my father, Dick Bauer, for his continued love and encouragement. He has also given me an appreciation for dedication, perseverance, and striving for excellence. I also thank Amy and Mary for their ongoing love and support. I look forward to seeing the paths taken by Jake, Sophia, Joshua, Grant, and Lucy; they have incredible parents. Thanks to Don, Ruth, and Brenda for all of their encouraging words.

—**Richard**

About the Authors

Julie R. Dahlquist, Ph.D., CMT is a senior lecturer, Department of Finance, at the University of Texas at San Antonio College of Business. She is the recipient of the 2011 Charles H. Dow Award for excellence and creativity in technical analysis. She is the coauthor (with Charles Kirkpatrick) of *Technical Analysis: The Complete Resource for Financial Market Technicians* and coauthor (with Richard Bauer) of *Technical Market Indicators: Analysis and Performance*. Her research has appeared in a number of publications, including *Financial Analysts Journal*, *Journal of Technical Analysis*, *Active Trader*, *Working Money*, *Managerial Finance*, *Financial Practices and Education*, and the *Journal of Financial Education*. She serves on the board of the Market Technicians Association Educational Foundation and is a frequent presenter at national and international conferences. She earned her B.B.A. and Ph.D. in economics from University of Louisiana at Monroe and Texas A&M, respectively, and her M.A. in Theology from St. Mary's University.

Richard J. Bauer, Jr., Ph.D., CFA, CMT is Professor of Finance at the Bill Greehey School of Business at St. Mary's University in San Antonio, Texas. His degrees include a B.S. in Physics, M.S. in Physics, M.S. in Economics, and a Ph.D. in Finance. He is the author of *Genetic Algorithms and Investment Strategies* and *Technical Market Indicators* (with J. Dahlquist*)*, both published by John Wiley and Sons. He is the recipient of the 2011 Charles H. Dow Award for excellence and creativity in technical analysis. His research has appeared in a number of publications, including *Financial Analysts Journal, Journal of Business Research, Managerial Finance*, and *Korean Financial Management Journal*. He became a CFA charterholder in 1990 and a CMT charterholder in 2010. He is a past president of the CFA Society of San Antonio.

Chapter 1

What Are Gaps?

Gaps have attracted the attention of market technicians since the earliest days of stock charting. A gap occurs when a security's price jumps between two trading periods, skipping over certain prices. A gap creates a hole, or a void, on a price chart.

Because technical analysis has traditionally been an extremely visual practice, it is easy to understand why early technicians noticed gaps. Gaps are visually conspicuous on a price chart. Consider, for example, the stock chart for Huntington Bancshares (HBAN) in Figure 1.1. A quick glance at the price activity reveals four gaps.

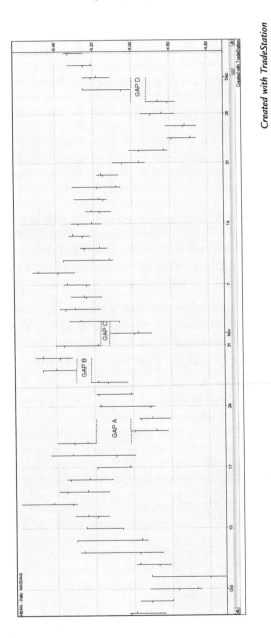

FIGURE 1.1   Gaps on stock chart for HBAN September 29–December 2, 2011

In Figure 1.1, Gap A and Gap C are known as a gap down. A **gap down** occurs when one day's high is lower than the previous day's low. In the figure you can see that the lowest price for HBAN on September 19 was $5.20. On September 20, the highest price at which HBAN traded was $5.01. Thus, a gap of 19 cents was formed. From September 19 through September 20, HBAN traded for $5.20 and higher and for $5.01 and lower; however, no shares traded hands at a price between $5.01 and $5.20. Thus, a void or gap in price was formed.

Just as a security's price can gap down, it can gap up. A gap up occurs when one day's low is greater than the previous day's high. Both Gaps B and D in Figure 1.1 represent gap ups.

Early technicians did not pay attention to gaps simply because they were conspicuous and easy to spot on a stock chart. Because gaps show that a price has jumped, they may represent some significant change in what is happening with the stock and present a trading opportunity.

A technical analyst watches stock price behavior, searching for signs of any change in behavior. If a stock is in a strong uptrend, the analyst watches for any sign that the trend has ended. When a stock is in a consolidation period, the analyst watches for any sign of a change in behavior that would indicate a breakout either to the upside or to the downside. Spotting these changes leads to profitable trading, allowing the trader to jump on a trend, ride the trend, and exit once the trend has ended. Gaps can be one indication of an impending change in trend.

Given the persistence of superstitions, such as "a gap must be closed," surprisingly little study has been undertaken to analyze the effectiveness of using gaps in trading. This book provides a comprehensive study of gaps in an attempt to isolate gaps which present profitable trading strategies.

Types of Gaps

Gap types differ based on the context in which they occur. Some price gaps are meaningful, and others can be disregarded.

Breakaway (or Breakout) Gaps

A **breakaway gap** is one that occurs at the beginning of a trend (see Figure 1.2). In November 2006, AT&T (T) was in a trading range. On November 29, the stock gapped up and an uptrend began. Because profits are made by jumping on and riding a trend, breakaway gaps are considered the most profitable gaps for trading purposes.

Runaway (or Measuring) Gaps

A gap that occurs along a trend line is called a **runaway gap** or a **measuring gap**. Often, a runaway gap appears in a strong trend that has few minor corrections. The contrast between a breakaway gap and a runaway gap is highlighted in Figure 1.3. In July 2006, Apple (AAPL) experienced a breakaway gap, with price jumping from $55 to $60 a share, and an uptrend began. The stock price headed higher over the next 3 months. Then, on October 19, the stock gapped up again by several dollars; the uptrend continued.

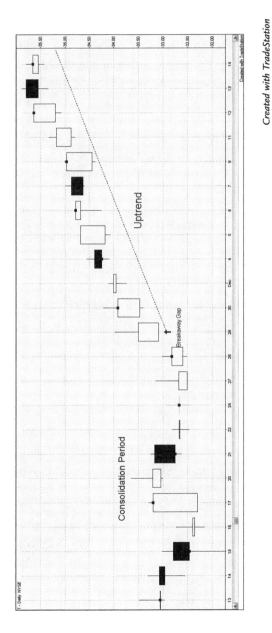

FIGURE 1.2 *Breakaway gap on stock chart for T, November 13–December 14, 2006*

Runaway gaps are often referred to as measuring gaps because of their tendency to occur at about the middle of a price run. Indeed, this is what AAPL did in Figure 1.3. Thus, the distance from the beginning of the trend to the runaway gap can be projected above the gap to obtain a target price. Bulkowski (2010) finds that an upward runaway gap occurs, on average, 43% of the distance from the beginning of the trend to the eventual peak, and a downward gap occurs, on average, at 57% of the distance.

Exhaustion Gaps

As its name sounds, an **exhaustion gap** occurs at the end of a trend. In the case of an uptrend, price makes one last attempt to move higher on a last gasp of breath; however, the trend is exhausted, and the higher price cannot be sustained. For example, the gap up on January 9, 2007 (refer to Figure 1.3) occurs as AAPL's powerful uptrend is coming to an end. It is easy to detect an exhaustion gap in hindsight; however, distinguishing an exhaustion gap from a runaway gap at the time of the gap can be difficult because the two share many characteristics.

Popular wisdom suggests that trading exhaustion gaps can be dangerous. An exhaustion gap signals the end of a trend. However, one of two things can happen; the trend may reverse immediately, or price may remain in a congestion area for some time. An exhaustion gap signals a trader to exit a position but does not necessarily signal the beginning of a new trend in the opposite position.

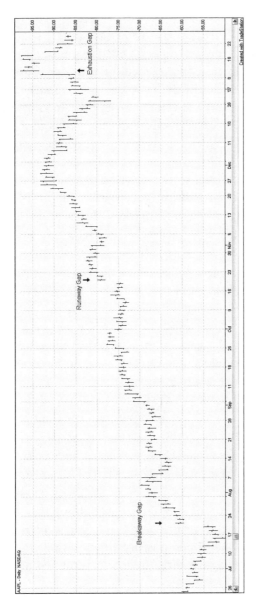

Created with TradeStation

FIGURE 1.3 *Runaway gap on stock chart for AAPL, June 23, 2006–January 24, 2007*

Other Gaps

In addition to breakaway, runaway, and exhaustion gaps, technical analysts identify a few types of gaps that are generally of no consequence for a trader. **Common gaps** occur in illiquid trading vehicles, are small in relation to the price of the vehicle, or appear in short-term trading data. An **ex-dividend gap** may occur in a stock price when a dividend is paid and the stock price is adjusted the following day. Ex-dividend gaps are insignificant, and the trader must be careful not to misinterpret them. **Suspension gaps** can occur in 24-hour futures trading when one market closes and another opens, especially if one market is electronic and the other is open outcry; these are also insignificant.

An **opening gap** occurs when the opening price for the day is outside the previous day's range. After the opening, price might continue to move in the direction of the gap, forming a gap for the day. Or the price might retrace, closing the gap. Figure 1.4 shows three opening gaps for McDonald's (MCD). See how, on December 2, MCD opened at a price higher than the December 1 price range. However, the price moved lower during the day, filling the gap, resulting in an overlap for the December 1 and December 2 bars.

Of course, any gap begins as an opening gap. On November 30 and December 8, MCD had an opening gap to the upside, and the price never retraced enough on those days to fill the gap. Throughout this book, when we use the term "gap" we are referring to instances in which the gap is not filled within the trading session unless we directly specify that we are discussing opening gaps.

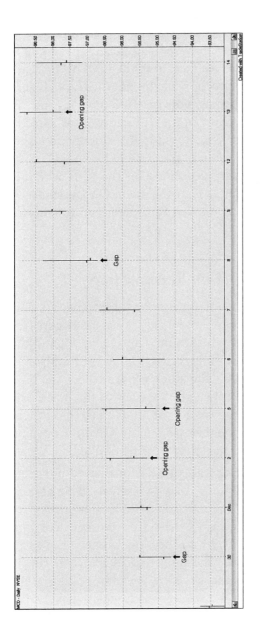

FIGURE 1.4   *Opening gap on stock chart for MCD, November 29–December 14, 2011*

Created with TradeStation

Some traders watch for trading opportunities with opening gaps. General wisdom suggests that if a gap is not filled within the first half hour, the odds of the trend continuing in the direction of the gap increase. Figure 1.4 showed an opening gap on December 2 and on December 5 for MCD. Figure 1.5 shows how quickly these opening gaps were closed by considering intraday data and using 5-minute bars. On December 2, for example, the opening was filled on the fifth 5-minute bar, or within 25 minutes of the open. On December 5, the opening gap was filled within the first 5 minutes of trading.

A Note on Terminology

This book focuses on daily charts and trading. To clarify, we use Day 0 to represent the day a gap occurs (see Figure 1.6). The day before the gap is Day –1 and the stock's high on Day –1 is the beginning of the gap. On the next day (Day 0), the stock's low exceeds the high on Day –1, forming the gap. We refer to the day of the gap as Day 0 because we do not know until the close of trading that day whether we simply have an opening gap or if we have a gap that remains unfilled.

If we are to make trading decisions based upon the occurrence of a gap, the soonest we would be able to enter a position is the open on Day 1. Thus, when we report a 1-day return, we base the return calculation from the open on Day 1 to the close on Day 1. To calculate longer returns, the return is calculated from the open at Day 1 to the close on the day of the return length; therefore, a 3-day return is calculated as buying at the open of Day 1 and selling at the close of Day 3.

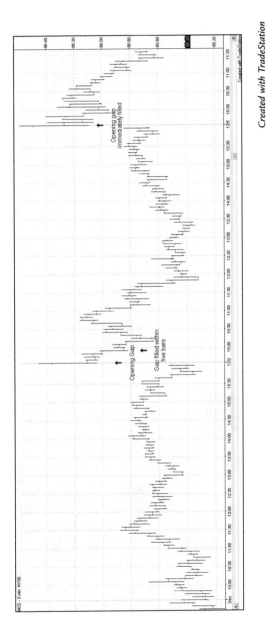

FIGURE 1.5 *Open gaps filled on intraday stock chart for MCD, December 1–5, 2011*

Created with TradeStation

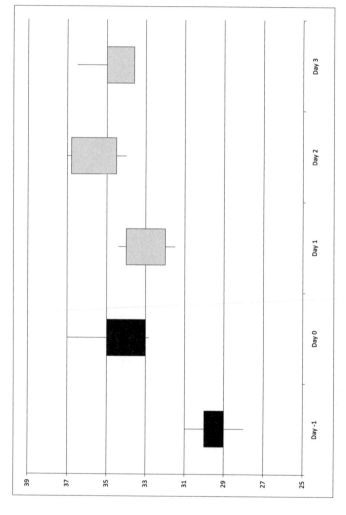

FIGURE 1.6   *Gap occurs on Day 0*

How to Use Gaps in Trading

How might a trader, seeing a gap, react to the information? If the trader thinks that the gap is a breakaway gap, he would want to trade in the direction of the gap. In other words, if a breakaway up gap occurred, he would assume an uptrend is beginning and take a long position. If a breakaway down gap occurred, he would assume a downtrend is beginning and take a short position. He would also want to trade in the direction of the gap, if the stock were trending and a gap occurred that he thought was a measuring gap. Throughout this book we refer to trading in the direction of the gap as a **continuation strategy** in that the trader is expecting the price to continue in the direction of the gap.

If a trader sees a gap she thinks drives the price up so much that there is little room for the price to push higher, she would want to trade opposite of the gap. Suppose, for example, a pharmaceutical company announces that it has received FDA approval for a new drug. Upon the release of this good news, the stock gaps up. If the trader thinks that the market is over-reacting to this good news, she would want to short the stock. Likewise, if she thinks that market players have driven the price down too low on a gap, she would want to take a long position. Remember the old adage that a gap must be filled. The notion that a gap is always filled is based on the idea that the market players do not like to see a hole or a void in a price movement and will work to fill that gap. We refer to trading in the opposite direction of a gap as a **reversal strategy**.

Traditional technical analysis theory would tell you to trade breakaway and measuring gaps using a continuation strategy. You might want to trade an exhaustion gap with a reversal strategy; however, a major problem is that traditional theory has not provided a sound way to classify a gap as it occurs. It is only in hindsight that you can tell if a gap was a breakaway, measuring, or exhaustion gap.

The main task in this book is to help you pick up on clues as to what type of gap may be occurring so that you can enter successful trades. Chapter 2, "Windows on Candlestick Charts," discusses traditional Japanese candlestick patterns that contain gaps. Chapter 3, "The Occurrence of Gaps," looks at the occurrence of gaps and considers the frequency of gaps, the distribution of gaps across stocks, and the distribution of gaps over time. Chapter 4, "How to Measure Returns," discusses our methodology for determining profitable gap trading strategies. Chapter 5, "Gaps and Previous Price Movement," considers what clues the price movement leading up to the gap gives you to form profitable trading strategies. Because volume is an indication of how important a particular day's price movement is, Chapter 6, "Gaps and Volume," considers the relationship between volume and gap profitability. To determine whether gaps that occur at relatively high prices have a different significance than those occurring at average or relatively low prices, Chapter 7, "Gaps and Moving Averages," considers the location of gaps relative to the price moving average. Although most of this book focuses on individual securities, you can look at the relationship between gap significance and underlying stock market activity in Chapter 8, "Gaps and the Market." Chapter 9, "Closing the Gap," covers the often-heard phrase, "A gap must be closed." Last,

Chapter 10, "Putting It All Together," provides an overall summary of how gaps can be used as part of an effective trading and investment strategy.

Endnotes

Bulkowski, Thomas N. "Bulkowski's Free Pattern Research," http://www.thepatternsite.com, 2010.

Chapter 2

Windows on Candlestick Charts

Now that we have covered the basics of what gaps are, let's look at how gaps are viewed on Japanese candlestick charts. **Japanese candlestick charts** display the same information (open, high, low, and close) that bar charts display but in a more striking way visually. Also, special vocabulary often accompanies the candlestick charts. For example, in Japanese candlestick charts, a gap is referred to as a **window**.

The candlestick chart of Johnson & Johnson (JNJ) in Figure 2.1 shows gaps, or windows, at points A, B, and C. For a window to occur, there must not be any overlap between two adjacent candles. For a window to occur, space must exist between the shadows of adjacent candles; because of this space, windows are also known as **disjointed candles**. In Figure 2.1, the real bodies of the candles on April 14 and April 15 do not overlap, but the shadows overlap; thus, a window does not occur.

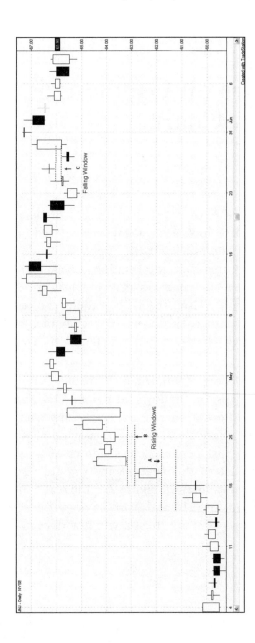

FIGURE 2.1   *Rising and falling windows, candlestick chart for JNJ, April 4–June 8, 2011*

A gap up is referred to as a **rising window**. Windows A and B are examples of rising windows (refer to Figure 2.1). In his book, *Japanese Candlestick Charting Techniques*,[1] Steve Nison states that Japanese technicians view windows as continuation signals and say to "go in the direction of the window." Thus, rising windows are considered bullish. When, a window occurs with a large white candle (refer to Window B in Figure 2.1), it is a **running window** because the market is said to be running in the direction of the window.

A down gap, such as the gap that occurs at Point C in Figure 2.1, is known as a **falling window**. Falling windows are considered bearish.

Candlestick Charting Basics

Although candlestick charts have been widely used in the Far East as early as the mid-1600s, the technique was relatively unknown to Western traders until the publication of the book *Japanese Candlestick Charting Techniques* by Steve Nison in 1989. Candlestick charts are similar to bar charts in that they are constructed using the high, low, and closing price. In addition, candlestick charts always include the opening price, something not always present on a bar chart. A rectangular box is created using the opening and closing prices, forming the *real body* of the candle. If the close exceeds the open, the real body is "white" or "open." If the close is lower than the open, the real body is "closed" and shaded black. Thin vertical bars, known as *shadows*, represent the high and low for the session.

Closing the window is simply filling a gap. Refer to Figure 2.1 to see that the falling Window C is closed the following day. For a window to be closed, the real body of a candle must close beyond the window,[2] as shown in Figure 2.2 for CROX. A falling window occurs on March 15. The upper shadow of the March 28 candle rises above the window; however, the real body still lies within the window. The window is not closed until 2 days later when the real body of the March 30 candlestick closes beyond the gap.

Some Japanese traders claim that if a window is not closed within three sessions, it is confirmation that the market should continue to move in the direction of the window. These traders see these unfilled windows as an indication that the market has the power to continue its trend for 13 more sessions. In his book *Beyond Candlesticks*,[3] Nison questions the preciseness of this claim but supports the notion of waiting three sessions for confirmation of a price trend (p. 100).

Windows as Support and Resistance

In candlestick charts, rising windows become support zones, and falling windows become resistance zones. Thus, you hear Japanese candlestick chart analysts stating that "Corrections stop at the window." Look, for example, at the September 1 rising window in Figure 2.3 (ATVI). The price initially moves higher in the direction of the rising window. However, on September 16, the price falls into the support zone. The price approaches but does not close below the 10.75 August 31 high. Because the window is not closed, traders can use this correction as a buying opportunity.

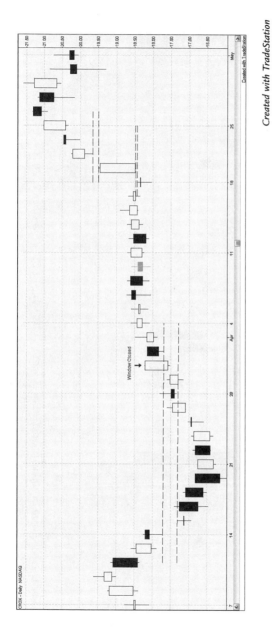

FIGURE 2.2   *Closing the window, candlestick chart for CROX, March 7—May 1, 2011*

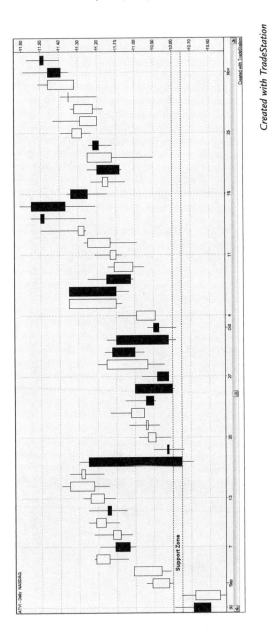

FIGURE 2.3   *A gap as support, candlestick chart for ATVI, August 30–November 2, 2010*

Created with TradeStation

Remember that a window can be large or small. A one-point rising window is still a window and serves as a support zone. According to Nison, the size of a window does not impact the importance of the window's role as a support or resistance zone. However, a large window has the disadvantage of creating a large zone. What does seem to be a factor in determining the importance of the zone is the trading volume for the gap candle. Heavy volume tends to enhance the effectiveness of window support and resistance zones.[4]

Traditional Japanese technical analysts place particular importance on the occurrence of three up (or three down) windows. After three up windows occur, the market is probably overbought; and after three down windows occur, the market is probably oversold. As shown in Figure 2.4, these windows do not need to occur on consecutive days. Three unclosed rising windows occurring during an uptrend would suggest an overbought market. Nison suggests that this idea comes from the emphasis that Japanese place on the number 3. In his experience, traders should consider the uptrend in place until the most recent window is closed rather than as soon as the third window rises. Refer to Figure 2.4 to see four rising windows. However, the fourth window is immediately closed, suggesting that the uptrend has come to an end.

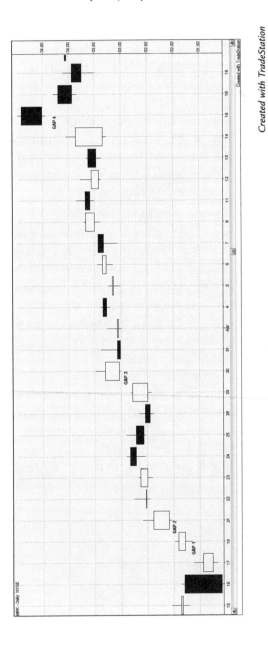

FIGURE 2.4   *Four rising windows, candlestick chart for MRK, March 15–April 19, 2011*

Created with TradeStation

Remember that, in general, a rising window is bullish and a falling window is bearish. This is especially true with high-price and low-price gapping plays. Figure 2.5 portrays a high-price gapping play for Krispy Kreme Donuts (KKD). An advance in price of about 18% at the beginning of May is followed by a consolidation period. This consolidation period is composed of small-bodied candlesticks and signals a period of market indecision. The breakout from the consolidation occurs on a rising window, which is viewed as bullish. Indeed, the price of KKD continued to advance through June to $10 a share.

A low-price gapping play is simply the reverse of the high-price gapping play. A downtrend is followed by a period of small-bodied candles. During this consolidation period it appears that a base may be forming. However, a bearish falling window indicates that this was not the case, and the downward trend in price should resume.

Candlestick Patterns Containing Windows

Although many candlestick patterns have Western equivalents, some patterns are unique to candlestick charting. These patterns often have intriguing names stemming from their Japanese heritage. Most candlestick patterns are short term and composed of one to five bars. Patterns are defined by the relative position of the body and shadow of a candlestick and the location of a candlestick in relation to its neighbors. Candlestick patterns that contain windows within the pattern are described below.

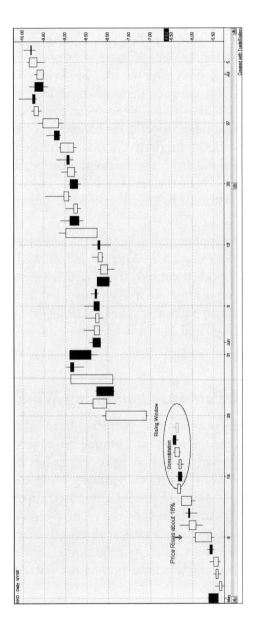

FIGURE 2.5   High-price gapping play, candlestick chart for KKD, May 1–July 5, 2011

Tasuki

The **tasuki** is a two-candle pattern. The **upward gapping tasuki** is composed of a rising window created by a white candle followed by a black candle that has a real body top that lies below the close of the previous session's close. The real bodies for the two candles are about the same size. Figure 2.6 shows an upward gapping tasuki for Tyco (TYC) that occurred December 1, 2011.

The **downward gap tasuki** is simply the reverse of the upward gapping tasuki. Figure 2.7 shows a downward gapping tasuki for Pearson (PSO). First, a black candle on August 18 creates a falling window. Second, a white candle occurs on August 19 with a real body about the same size as the black candle's real body. The real body low for this white candle lies above the close for the black body candle. The real bodies of the August 18 and August 19 candles are roughly the same size, and the window is not closed by the August 19 white candle.

The tasuki candlestick pattern is identified by the colors, relative sizes, and relative positions of the candlesticks on the day of and the day following the window. However, these characteristics do not appear to have a significant impact on the importance of the window. The significant items are the direction of the window and whether the window is closed. Thus, although interesting for informational purposes, identifying the tasuki pattern in not extremely useful to a trader.

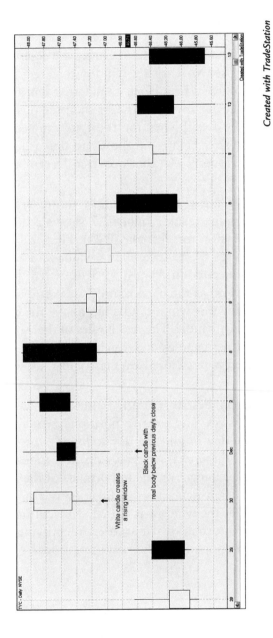

FIGURE 2.6   Upward gapping tasuki, candlestick chart for TYC, November 28–December 13, 2011

Created with TradeStation

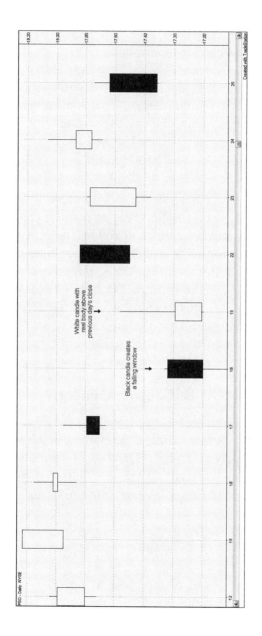

FIGURE 2.7   *Downward gapping tasuki, candlestick chart for PSO, August 12–25, 2011*

Gapping Side-by-Side White Lines

The **upgap side-by-side white lines** pattern is created when, during an uptrend, a window occurs with a white candle. The following session is also a white candle of similar size, with a similar open. This is a bullish continuation pattern. Again, the unclosed rising window by itself would be bullish. The two white candles reinforce this bullish signal, as shown in Figure 2.8.

The extremely rare **downgap side-by-side white lines** pattern begins when a downtrend contains a falling window with a white candle, creating a down gap. The next session is also a white candle. The adjacent white candles that compose the side-by-side white lines are of similar size and similar open. Also, the second white candle cannot close the window. Because the window is a falling window, this pattern is viewed as bearish despite the existence of two white candles. The white candles are assumed to be short covering, and the downtrend is expected to continue.

Two Black Gapping Candles

If a downside gap is followed by two black candles rather than two white candles, the pattern is known as **two black gapping candles**. The falling window is a bearish indicator by itself. When it is followed by two black candles, it is viewed as even more bearish.

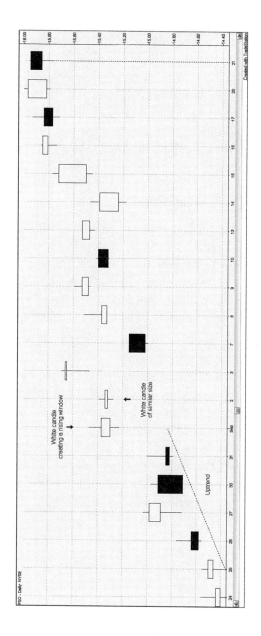

FIGURE 2.8   *Upgap side-by-side white lines, candlestick chart for PSO, August 24–September 21, 2010*

Created with TradeStation

Figure 2.9 illustrates the two black gapping candles pattern that occurred for BP in May 2010. BP was in a strong downtrend when a black candle created a falling window on May 14. The next trading day, May 17, another black candle formed; this second black candle had a similar open to the May 14 candle. As this bearish indicator would suggest, the stock price continued to fall, resulting in a decline in price of approximately 10% over the next week.

Gapping Doji

The **gapping doji** is just what its name sounds like: a window that is created by a doji. A **doji** is a candle with no real body, meaning that the opening price and closing price for the session are identical. A gapping doji appearing during a downtrend is considered bearish. The gapping doji is another pattern that is rarely seen.

Although the traditional Japanese materials mention the gapping doji only in a downtrend, Nison (*Beyond Candlesticks*, p. 106) suggests that there is no reason to believe that the same logic would not apply to gapping dojis in uptrends. In addition, Nison recommends waiting for confirmation of a continued downtrend in the session after the window; a long, white candle that trades higher in the following session would create a bullish morning star pattern that would negate the negative signal of the gapping doji.

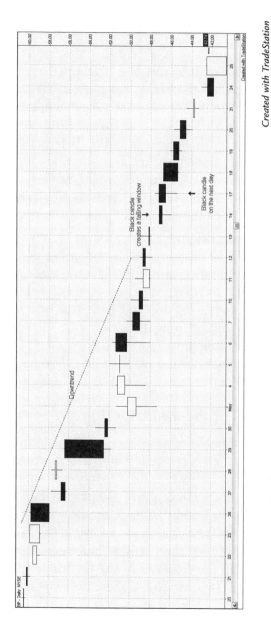

Created with TradeStation

FIGURE 2.9   *Two black gapping candles, candlestick chart for BP, April 20–May25, 2010*

Collapsing Doji Star

The **collapsing doji star** is a bearish pattern that contains two windows. It begins at a high price level as a white candle pushes the price even higher. The session after the white candle is a doji that gaps down, creating a falling window. The next session creates another falling window with a black candle. This pattern is known as the "omen of a large decline" among Japanese candlestick chartists. (*Beyond Candlesticks*, p. 115) A collapsing doji star occurred on November 8, 2010 for RBS stock, as shown in Figure 2.10.

The collapsing doji star is an extremely rare pattern. We found only 89 instances of a collapsing doji star over the 30-year time period of 1982 through 2011.[5] Although that averages out to approximately 3 instances of a collapsing doji star each year, you might spend a long time waiting and watching for one to occur. One occurred July 5, 1990 for Ericsson (ERIC) and another did not occur until March 8, 1996 for Tyco (TYC).

Abandoned Baby Top

The **abandoned baby top** is a three-candle pattern. It is a special case of an evening doji star. The evening doji star is composed of a white candle, followed by a doji with the real body lying above the real body of the white candle, followed by a black candle with the real body lying below the real body of the doji. For the abandoned baby top, the bottom shadow of the doji does not overlap the shadows of the first or third candles, resulting in two windows. These two windows are shown in Figure 2.11 for RBS.

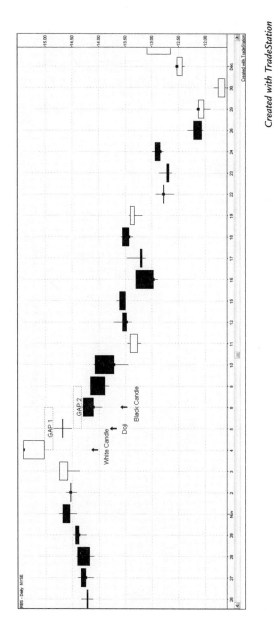

FIGURE 2.10   *Collapsing doji star, candlestick chart for RBS, October 26–December 1, 2010*

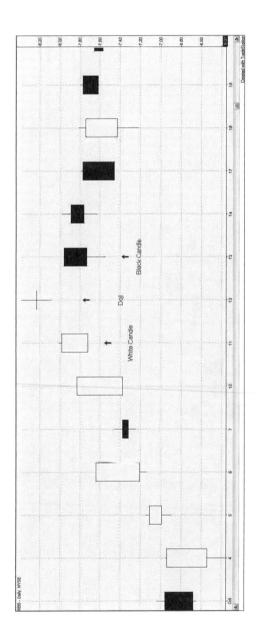

FIGURE 2.11   Abandoned baby top, candlestick chart for RBS, October 3–October 19, 2011

Created with TradeStation

This top reversal signal is rare. Only 299 occurred during the study period of 1950 through 2011. However, the abandoned baby top has been more prevalent in recent years. About half of the abandoned baby tops observed over the 60-year study period were in the last decade. Twenty-three occurred in 2010 and 18 occurred in 2011, accounting for approximately 14% of the abandoned baby tops in the past 60 years.

Abandoned Baby Bottom

Like the abandoned baby top, the reverse pattern, an **abandoned baby bottom** is extremely rare. During the 1950–2011 study period, 320 abandoned baby bottoms existed. Only two abandoned baby bottoms occurred before 1980, both in 1974. However, 16 of the abandoned baby bottoms occurred in 2010, and another 32 of the abandoned baby bottoms occurred in 2011. Thus, 15% of the abandoned baby bottoms occurring during the past 60 years have been seen in the past 2 years.

An abandoned baby bottom for Hasbro (HAS) is shown in Figure 2.12. The first candle in this pattern is black. The second candle is a doji, and the shadow of the doji lies completely below the shadow of the first candle, creating a window. The third candle is white, with the shadow completely above the shadow of the doji, creating a second window. (Nison, p. 70)

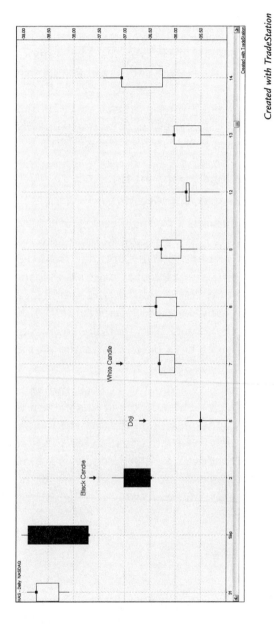

Created with TradeStation

FIGURE 2.12   *Abandoned baby bottom, candlestick chart for HAS, August 31–September 14, 2011*

Trading with Windows

Candlestick patterns are tools, not a system. The significance of many of the patterns depends upon previous price movement. To determine how meaningful a pattern is, the analyst must often consider whether it occurs during an uptrend, downtrend, or a sideways move in the market.

In addition, some of these patterns are extremely rare. The more bars included in the pattern, the more constraints put on the construction of each bar, and the more constraints put on the relative positions of the bars, the less frequent a pattern will be.

Thomas Bulkowski maintains a Web site that contains information about a number of technical patterns, including 103 candlestick patterns (www.thepatternsite.com). Searching through almost 5 million candlesticks, Bulkowski provides statistics about the frequency and performance of candlestick patterns. In general, Bulkowski's results are not that favorable for this subset of candlestick patterns.

The best performing of the patterns containing windows is the upward gapping tasuki. The upward gapping tasuki ranks 4th among the 103 candlestick patterns, according to Bulkowski's performance measurements. Unfortunately, this pattern is rare; Bulkowski finds only 704 instances of the upward gapping tasuki in 4.7 million candlesticks. Another pattern that performs reasonably well (9th out of 103) is the abandoned baby bottom. However, an abandoned baby bottom is even rarer than the upward gapping tasuki; the abandoned baby bottom is ranked 92 out of 103 patterns for its frequency. The collapsing doji star is even rarer;

Bulkowski finds only 16 examples of the pattern. At this rate, he points out, a trader using minute bars would find a collapsing doji star only once every 3.3 years!

Bulkowski finds that the two black gapping candles pattern occurs more frequently than other window containing patterns; out of the 103 candlestick patterns he considered, the two black candles pattern is the 29th most common pattern. The pattern also ranks 10th for how well it performs relative to other candlestick patterns.

Although patterns with names such as "abandoned baby bottom" garner much attention, looking at the traditional window-containing patterns has not seemed to be exceptionally beneficial to traders. The rarity of these patterns not only means that a trader must wait a long time watching for some of them, but it also calls into question the validity of the results you see for the patterns. As you go through the remainder of the book looking at how gaps can be traded, you will encounter some of the candlestick terminology and look at some nontraditional ways that candle colors and patterns might be helpful in the development of a successful trading strategy.

Endnotes

1. Nison, Steve. *Japanese Candlestick Charting Techniques*. New York, NY: New York Institute of Finance, 2001.

2. The terminology of "closing a window" is used in Japanese candlestick charting in a slightly different

way than "closing a gap" in traditional technical analysis. When any price movement totally fills the void on a bar chart, the gap is said to be closed. With a candlestick chart, the window is closed only if the body of a candle fills the gap. Thus, in traditional bar chart analyses, the gap in Figure 2.2 would be said to be closed on March 28. Because this chapter discusses Japanese candlestick patterns, we use the Japanese definition of closing a window when referring to gaps in this chapter.

3. Nison, Steve. *Beyond Candlesticks*. New York, NY: John Wiley & Sons, 1994.

4. We will examine the impact that gap size and trading volume have on trading performance in depth in future chapters. This chapter focuses on the ways in which gaps are generally viewed by those who analyze traditional candlestick chart patterns.

5. The search period begins in 1950; no collapsing dojis exist for the stocks in this study prior to 1982.

Chapter 3

The Occurrence of Gaps

This chapter examines the frequency of gaps across many dimensions. How often do gaps occur? Are gaps becoming more frequent or less frequent over time? Does index membership play a role in gap frequency? This chapter explores these questions.

Data and Software

Before getting into the answers to those questions, you need to understand the data used in writing this book. The stock data came from Norgate Investor Services, which sells a software package called Premium Data. There are two different U.S. stock price datasets available within Premium Data. Historical data can be purchased for either currently listed stocks or delisted stocks. The base package for each contains price history from 1985, but an add-on extends the price history to 1950.

You can find details concerning the database methodology and a discussion of delisting on the Premium Data Web site (www.premiumdata.net/products/premiumdata/ushistorical.php#delisted). The prices have been adjusted for splits, reverse splits, and other capital-related corporate actions. Adjusting for splits causes prices to be adjusted backward in time to provide a continuous series from a value perspective. For example, a 2 for 1 stock split should cause a stock's price to drop in half (in the absence of other information). So if before the split you owned 100 shares at $50 per share, after the split you would own 200 shares at $25 per share. Obviously, the value of your stock holdings is not down by 50%. To avoid the appearance of a 50% drop in value, the pre-split price is adjusted to $25. This price adjustment is continued backward in time to the beginning of the price data.

The price adjustment previously described can cause some confusion. Say that this book describes prices around the occurrence of a gap that occurred sometime in 2002. If you were to refer to price charts, price quotes, newspaper articles, web discussions, and so on at the time of the actual gap, the price may be different than what this book uses due to price adjustments that have been made to keep continuity in the series. Although price adjustments affect the quoted numbers, they do not affect the identification of gaps or percentage changes (such as investment returns). If the open, high, low, and close prices have all been adjusted by the same factor, a gap between numbers such as 50 and 52 is still a gap if the numbers have been adjusted to 25 and 26. Furthermore, the percentage difference between the two numbers is 4% in both cases.

For purposes of this book, our dataset goes from 1995 through the end of 2011. (Later you will learn that 2011 was an interesting year for gaps.)[1] The ending date affects index membership and industry designation. It is extremely difficult to reconstruct index membership over time. Because index membership vis-à-vis gaps is interesting, but not critical, we opted to simply use index membership and industry designations as of the end of 2011.

Liquidity Considerations

Liquidity is a tricky issue to handle. Suppose you use software that helps you identify stock price gaps, and you see that a certain stock has gapped up on a certain date. Examining more closely, you see that the price gap was from $1.02 to $1.03 and that the total trading volume for the 2 days was 5,000 shares. Would this be of interest? Unless you were an individual investor with limited funds, probably not. A dollar volume of trading of approximately $5,000 over a 2-day period for most investors would be woefully inadequate liquidity. What if the price gap were from $102 to $103 and the total trading volume were 50,000,000 shares? Would this be adequate liquidity? For almost all investors the answer would be "Yes." But, the two examples are radically different. What about examples that fall between these two?

In trying to determine a reasonable liquidity constraint, we talked to various experienced market professionals. We got a variety of opinions about what numbers should be used to impose a liquidity constraint concerning which gaps to include in our study. In the end, we opted to impose a constraint that the dollar-volume of trading (closing price times shares traded) had to be at least $5,000,000 on the day of the gap and the two preceding days. Therefore, a stock trading at approximately $5 per share with a trading volume of 500,000 shares per day would not have made the cut. But if the price had been approximately $10 per share with volume of 500,000 shares per day, it would have made the cut. In addition, we also imposed a separate volume constraint of 100,000 shares per day.

The $5 million dollar-volume and 100,000 shares per day volume criteria seemed reasonable for 2011, but what about earlier years? We experimented with various approaches to adjust the two constraints in earlier years. There seemed to be some problems with every approach; there isn't any perfect way to make such an adjustment. In the end, we opted to make a linear adjustment based on the number of years prior to 2011. After examining the total number of gaps relative to the number of stocks listed at the time and examining which stocks were included or excluded at various points in time, we arrived at an adjustment that we felt was reasonable.[2]

Frequency of Gaps

So, how frequently do gaps occur? Table 3.1 shows the total number of gaps by year for currently listed stocks. As shown, there is no shortage of gaps to examine. In 2010, 22,936 gaps occurred; in 2011, this number increased to 32,232. A logical question from a trading perspective is, "How many gap trading opportunities am I going to have on an average day?" Because the total number of gaps has been increasing fairly steadily over the years, you could just take a daily average using the most recent year as an estimate of what you might expect. The number of trading days in a year varies slightly from year to year, but 252 is an average often used. With that in mind, the 32,232 gaps in 2011 divided by 252 gives an average of about 128 gaps per trading day. Clearly, it would seem that potential trading opportunities are frequent occurrences.

TABLE 3.1　*Frequency of Gaps by Year, 1995–2011*

Year	Down	Up	Total Gaps
1995	1,274	1,772	3,046
1996	1,777	2,260	4,037
1997	2,237	3,335	5,572
1998	3,219	4,026	7,245
1999	2,863	4,452	7,315
2000	4,024	4,933	8,957
2001	4,907	4,970	9,877
2002	4,936	5,390	10,326
2003	3,978	6,344	10,322
2004	5,186	6,300	11,486
2005	5,072	7,117	12,189
2006	6,308	8,659	14,967
2007	7,578	9,862	17,440
2008	9,244	7,662	16,906
2009	8,360	10,719	19,079
2010	9,973	12,963	22,936
2011	16,093	16,139	32,232
Total	97,029	116,903	213,932

However, the situation is more complicated due to clumping. Gaps are not evenly distributed across the year. The number of gaps can be extremely high on certain days, which leads to some other questions addressed shortly.

Table 3.2 shows the 25 days with the highest number of gaps. It is quite interesting that the 9 days with the highest number of gaps all occurred in 2011 and that 14 of the top 25 were in 2011. There was much discussion in 2011 about the high degree of market volatility. The high incidence of extreme gap days was another manifestation of market volatility.

TABLE 3.2   *Days with the Greatest Number of Gaps, 1995–2011*

Rank	Date	Total Gaps	Gaps Down	Gaps Up
1	8/18/2011	1,277	1,276	1
2	9/22/2011	1,160	1,159	1
3	11/30/2011	1,066	1	1,065
4	9/7/2011	1,040	3	1,037
5	9/2/2011	1,032	1,025	7
6	8/29/2011	958	—	958
7	11/1/2011	951	949	2
8	10/27/2011	891	9	882
9	9/27/2011	808	1	807
10	6/29/2010	784	784	—
11	8/11/2010	711	711	—
12	10/6/2008	706	706	—
13	2/17/2009	653	649	4
14	11/21/2011	645	644	1
15	4/2/2009	627	—	627
16	11/28/2011	627	1	626
17	12/1/2010	623	6	617
18	4/20/2011	599	3	596
19	3/30/2009	582	582	—
20	5/23/2011	579	579	—
21	2/27/2007	566	563	3
22	9/6/2011	563	562	1
23	8/24/2010	554	554	—
24	6/1/2009	553	—	553
25	4/9/2009	553	4	549

Now think about some reasons that gaps might occur. You can divide the reasons into three categories: marketwide events, industry-specific events, and company-specific events. Some events that may have broad market impact are political events, acts of war/terrorism, commodity price shocks (especially oil), interest rate changes, and currency changes. For these events to have substantial market impact, they would need to be unexpected events.

Things like the election results concerning the 2008 election would not be totally unexpected. The polling data leading into election day suggested that Obama was likely to be elected, so little market impact would be expected when the expected occurred. On the day of the election, November 4, there were 116 up gaps and 9 down gaps. On the following day, there were 39 down gaps and 3 up gaps, not a high amount of activity. What about the 2000 Bush-Gore election with its chaotic Florida recount? The gap activity on November 8, the day after the election, was minimal; there were 39 down gaps and 3 up gaps.

Compare these events to a virtually unexpected event such as the tragedy of 9/11. Because the attacks occurred in the early morning, the New York markets had not yet opened that Tuesday. Due to the damage in New York City, the New York Stock Exchange, the American Stock Exchange, and the NASDAQ remained closed until Monday, September 17. The gap activity when markets reopened was a combination of marketwide and industry-specific effects. Three-hundred-and-twenty-one stocks gapped that Monday. Not surprisingly, most of the gaps, 310, were down gaps.

But, there were 11 stocks that gapped up. Five of the 11 were defense industry stocks (General Dynamics, L-3 Communication Holdings, Raytheon, Lockheed Martin, and Northrup Grumman).[3]

Some company-specific events that could cause gaps are mergers and acquisitions, court rulings, regulatory actions (such as approval of a drug), SEC actions, and changes in top management (such as the unexpected death of a CEO). An acquisition offer caused Taro Pharmaceutical (TAROF) to gap up (see Figure 3.1) on October 18, 2011. Besides possible acquisitions, pharmaceutical companies are particularly prone to some large gaps when the results of drug trials are released. BioSante Pharma Inc. (BPAX) (see Figure 3.2) gapped down strongly on December 15, 2011 when news emerged that one of its drugs had failed Phase 3 clinical trials, which is the final testing phase. Figure 3.3 shows the large gap down for Avon Products (AVP) on October 27, 2011. This was triggered by the announcement that the SEC was investigating Avon concerning whether the company's contact with some financial analysts violated fair disclosure regulations.

Another question to ask is, "Are gaps more likely to occur on some days of the week rather than others?" You might hypothesize, for example, that more gaps would occur on Monday than other days of the week because 3 days of new information is incorporated into the price rather than just one. However, the information provided in Table 3.3 suggests that gaps occur with about the same frequency on Monday through Thursday, with Friday seeing slightly fewer gaps.

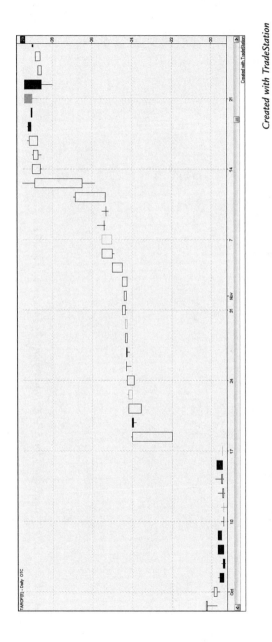

FIGURE 3.1   *Daily stock chart for TAROF, September 30–November 24, 2011*

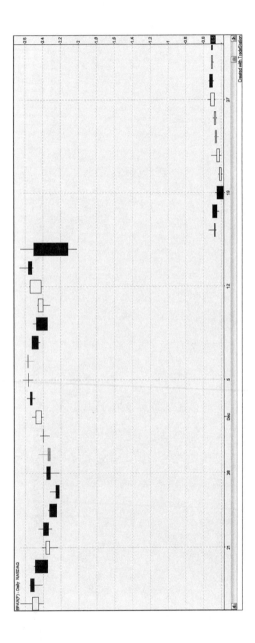

FIGURE 3.2   Daily stock chart for BPAX, November 17–December 30, 2011

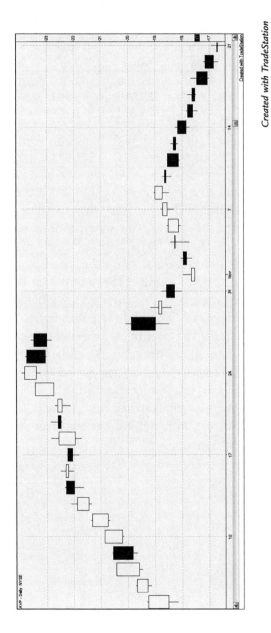

FIGURE 3.3   *Daily stock chart for AVP, October 3–November 21, 2011*

TABLE 3.3   *Occurrence of Gaps by Day of the Week, 1995-2011*

Day of the Week	Down Gaps	Up Gaps	Total Gaps	% of Gaps
Monday	18,715	25,200	43,915	20.53%
Tuesday	21,934	22,029	43,963	20.55%
Wednesday	17,916	24,872	42,788	20.00%
Thursday	21,024	23,557	44,581	20.84%
Friday	17,440	21,245	38,685	18.08%
Total	97,029	116,903	213,932	100.00%

Do gaps tend to occur in certain months more than other months? Table 3.4 presents the distribution of gaps by month. Of course, not every month has the same number of trading days. February, for example, often has fewer trading days than other months simply because it is a shorter month. The number of trading days in a given month is also affected by when weekends and holidays fall. The highest percentage of gaps (10.26%) occur in the month of September, whereas only 6.66% of the gaps occur in December. Approximately 21.5% of down gaps occur in September and October. April is an interesting month in that it has the highest percentage of up gaps of any month (10.5%) but is second lowest, only behind December in the percentage of down gaps.

TABLE 3.4 *Occurrences of Gaps by Month, 1995–2011*

Month	Down Gaps	Up Gaps	Total	% of Down Gaps	% of Up Gaps	% of Total Gaps
January	6,868	8,038	14,906	7.08%	6.88%	6.97%
February	7,220	7,463	14,683	7.44%	6.38%	6.86%
March	7,579	9,139	16,718	7.81%	7.82%	7.81%
April	6,596	12,279	18,875	6.80%	10.50%	8.82%
May	8,661	8,657	17,318	8.93%	7.41%	8.10%
June	8,282	8,675	16,957	8.54%	7.42%	7.93%
July	8,419	9,564	17,983	8.68%	8.18%	8.41%
August	9,987	8,954	18,941	10.29%	7.66%	8.85%
September	10,883	11,066	21,949	11.22%	9.47%	10.26%
October	8,502	12,117	20,619	8.76%	10.37%	9.64%
November	8,598	12,138	20,736	8.86%	10.38%	9.69%
December	5,434	8,813	14,247	5.60%	7.54%	6.66%

Size of Gaps

In addition to looking simply at the number of gaps, it is useful to examine gap size; all gaps are not created equally. Remember that a gap means that there is a jump in the movement of a security's price from one day to the next. A gap can be as small as a penny, or it can be as large as several dollars. There is theoretically no limit to the size of an up gap, but a stock's price can't fall more than 100%.

This raises the question of how to measure the size of the gap. The authors chose to look at the percentage size of the gap using a wick-to-wick (in candlestick terms) measure. For stocks that gapped up, calculate the percentage change from the previous day's high to the low on the day of the gap. In formula form, this is

$$\text{Up Gap Size} = \frac{(\text{Low for Day 0} - \text{High for Day } -1)}{\text{High for Day } -1}$$

For down gaps, calculate the percentage change from the previous day's low to the high on the day of the gap:

$$\text{Down Gap Size} = \frac{(\text{High for Day 0} - \text{Low for Day } -1)}{\text{Low for Day } -1}$$

The average (or mean) size of an up gap in the sample is 1.1052%. The average size of a down gap is −1.3394%. The vast majority of gaps are less than 1% either up or down. However, there are some extreme cases: Table 3.5 shows the five largest up gaps and down gaps over the 1995–2011 time period. The largest up gap in the database occurred on July 20, 2009, when Human Genome Sciences (HGSI) gapped up 150.69%.

As shown in Figure 3.4, HGSI had been trading between $2 and $4 a share since late May 2009. On July 20, the stock opened at a price of $10.89; even though the price fell to a low of $9.10 during the day, it closed near its high at $12.51, leaving a substantial hole, or gap, visible in the chart.

TABLE 3.5   *Largest Up Gaps and Down Gaps in %, 1995–2011*

Company Name	Ticker	Gap Size in %	Date Gap Occurred
Largest Up Gaps			
Human Genome Sciences	HGSI	150.69	July 20, 2009
Dendreon Co	DNDN	124.72	March 30, 2007
Dendreon Co	DNDN	102.53	April 14, 2009
Intermune Inc	ITMN	89.36	December 17, 2010
Clst Holdings	CLHI	77.78	June 25, 1998
Largest Down Gaps			
Lehman Brothers Holding	LEHMQ	−89.27	September 15, 2008
Keryx Biopharmaceuticals	KERX	−84.31	March 10, 2008
Amarin Corp	AMRN	−76.69	April 24, 2007
Intermune Inc	ITMN	−73.33	May 5, 2010
Biosante Pharma Inc	BPAX	−73.27	December 15, 2011

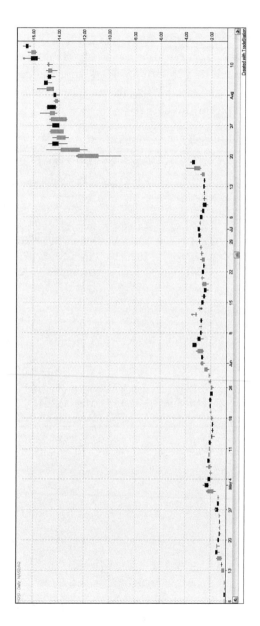

FIGURE 3.4   Largest gap up, daily stock chart for HGSI, April 6–August 13, 2009

Created with TradeStation

What happened that caused HGSI's stock to more than double in price from one trading day to the next? Business news headlines that day stated, "Shares of Human Genome Sciences Inc. rocketed on Monday after the company released a positive late stage study for its new lupus drug Benlysta, fueling speculation that it could be taken over by commercial partner GlaxoSmithKine." (Kennedy) This enormous gap occurred due to substantial company-specific news.

At the other end of the spectrum, the stock with the largest down gap will probably come as no surprise. On September 17, 2008, Lehman Brothers Holding Company (LEHMQ) dropped with a gap of more than 89%. Figure 3.5 shows the downward move in LEHMQ leading up to this enormous gap. As recently as February, the stock was trading at 65. By August the stock had dropped to 15. By September 9, the stock had fallen below 10, and 2 days later, on September 11, it was down below 5. It was like watching a limbo contest. How low could it go? On September 15, with the stock at approximately 20 cents per share, the company filed a petition under Chapter 11 of the U.S. bankruptcy code. Furthermore, on September 17, the NYSE moved to suspend trading of LEHMQ on the exchange.

Gaps by Index Membership and Industry

Another way to slice things is to view the data by index membership. The index membership is as of the end of 2011. So a stock that ended 2011 as one of the S&P 500 component stocks may not have been in the index during previous years.

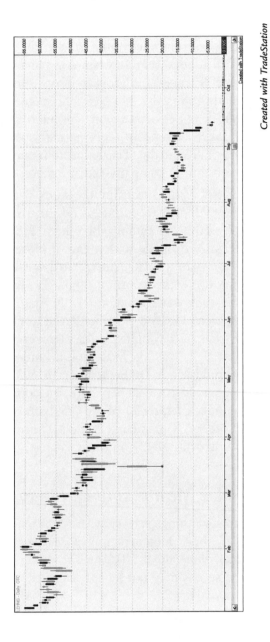

FIGURE 3.5   *Largest gap down, daily stock chart for LEHMQ, January 1—October 17, 2008*

Created with TradeStation

Market capitalization, often referred to as **market cap**, is a simplistic measure of a company's size. To find market cap, you multiple the company's stock price by the number of shares outstanding. The basic logic is, "How much would I have to pay to buy all the stock of the company?" However, this is a crude estimate. The observed price at a given point in time is the price for a transaction involving a limited number of shares (typically 100 to 10,000). If you want to buy all the shares, you would pay far more (as evidenced by tender offers) to attract more sellers.

The indexes differ by market cap, number of index components, and construction methodology (such as price-weighted or value-weighted). Some of our students have actually missed an exam bonus question (that was meant as a gift) that was stated as "How many stocks are in the S&P 500 (note: this is NOT a trick question)?"

Table 3.6 shows the total number of gaps and average gap sizes for various indexes focusing just on 2011. Because the index membership was determined at the end of 2011, the breakdown is fairly accurate. There were index component changes that occurred at various points in the year, but they would probably not have significantly affected the Table 3.6 patterns. The figures in Table 3.6 show a tendency for stocks with smaller market caps to have (on average) larger gaps. One conjecture is that it relates to liquidity. Think about Wal-Mart (WMT) versus TravelZoo (TZOO), a Russell Microcap stock. Wal-Mart is a component of both the

S&P 500 and the Dow Jones Industrial Average. WMT has a large analyst following and had an average volume of 17.3 million shares on the days it gapped in 2011. TZOO's average volume on the days it gapped was just under 2 million shares. The large number of eyes following WMT means that many people are aware of every small piece of news that might impact its price. Even a small news item might cause someone to initiate a trade. On the other hand, minor news related to TZOO may go unnoticed or may simply be ignored. This could lead to larger price jumps when an accumulation of news occurs, which would cause more price gapping.

Stocks also vary greatly in the number of gaps they experience. There were more than 9,000 stocks in the database of currently listed stocks. Of these there were 2,714 that experienced at least one gap (subject to price and volume constraints at the time of the gap) during the 1995–2011 time period. The average number of gaps per stock was 79. The median was 50.

Which stocks experienced the most gaps? Table 3.7 shows the ten stocks with the highest number of gaps. News Corp Ltd. (NWS), with 573 total gaps, had the most. Given the earlier discussion about how stock prices are affected by unexpected news, it is ironic that News Corp Ltd. had the highest number of gaps. Its pattern of gaps was reasonably consistent over time. It had at least 16 gaps in each of the 17 years from 1995 through 2011. The peak was in 2000 when it gapped 69 times.

TABLE 3.6 *Gap Occurrences in 2011 by Index Membership*

	Average Gap Size		Number of Down Gaps	Number of Up Gaps	Total Number of Gaps
	Down Gaps	Up Gaps			
DJIA	−0.8068	0.6548	402	397	799
SP500	−0.9381	0.7757	5,662	5,915	11,577
SP400	−1.0061	0.9313	3,492	3,435	6,927
SP600	−1.2139	1.1551	1,675	1,777	3,452
RU1000	−1.0005	0.8443	9,735	9,825	19,560
RU2000	−1.4202	1.2412	4,222	4,311	8,533
RU3000	−1.1275	0.9654	13,957	14,136	28,093
RUMid	−1.0439	0.8898	7,507	7,504	15,011
RUMicr	−2.7007	1.6273	391	372	763
NSDQ100	−1.2521	0.8653	868	968	1,836
CBOE	−1.1416	0.9659	13,675	13,811	27,486

TABLE 3.7   *Ten Stocks with the Highest Number of Gaps,*
1995–2011

Ticker	Name	Down Gaps	Up Gaps	Total
NWS	News Corp Ltd Class B	257	316	573
FRO	Frontline Ltd	204	226	430
NEM	Newmont Mining Cp	209	217	426
CCL	Carnival Corp	165	205	370
RCL	Royal Caribbean Cruise Ltd	154	198	352
MS	Morgan Stanley Dean Witter	155	195	350
C	Citigroup Inc	147	199	346
AA	Alcoa Inc	157	183	340
BA	Boeing Co	154	180	334
TXN	Texas Instruments	146	184	330

A final way to slice the number of gaps is by industry. The term "industry" seems straightforward at first blush. However, there are many complications. Is there such a thing as the "computer" industry? It is a term you might use in casual conversation. However, does it make sense to lump IBM, EA, and STX together? IBM engages in a wide range of activities from various types of software to various types of hardware to consulting services. Electronic Arts (EA) makes multimedia and graphics software. Seagate Technology PLC (STX) specializes in data storage devices. You could easily subdivide "computer industry" into multiple smaller industries. Who decides which industry a given company is in? There are a number of different classification schemes, some developed by private sources and some developed by public entities. Premium Data provides a classification scheme that assigns each company into one of 102 different industries (103 if you count "unclassified").

Table 3.8 lists the industries (the unclassified category is not shown in this list but would have ranked 2nd with 8,155 gaps) with the largest number of total gaps. The semiconductor industry accounted for 5.7% of all gaps; approximately 31% of all gaps occurred in one of these ten industries.

TABLE 3.8   *Industries with the Highest Number of Gaps, 1995–2011*

Industry	Down	Up	Total
Semiconductors	5,504	6,773	12,277
Exploration and Production	3,217	4,503	7,720
Oil Equipment & Services	2,985	3,923	6,908
Real Estate Investment Trusts	3,297	3,474	6,771
Software	2,987	3,693	6,680
Banks	3,044	3,228	6,272
Telecommunications Equipment	2,369	2,985	5,354
Electrical Components and Equipment	2,290	2,870	5,160
Electricity	2,240	2,384	4,624
Specialty Retailers	1,954	2,514	4,468

Do these results make sense? We think they do, at least in a general sense. It seems logical that stocks in industries sensitive to major marketwide events (such as oil price shocks) might have a high number of gaps. This would explain why the exploration and production industry, for example, is second in the list. Beyond marketwide factors some industries are just more volatile than others. For example, high-tech stocks are more volatile than consumer staple stocks.

Summary

Gaps can occur for a variety of reasons. There may be some macroeconomic event such as a sudden jump in the price of oil or the impact of a terrorist attack. Oil price changes affect some industries, such as airlines, more than other industries, so there are days when most of the gaps are concentrated in a few industries. At the individual company level there are many possible events that could lead to a gap in the company's stock price such as court decisions, mergers and acquisitions, regulatory rulings such as the results of pharmaceutical trials, and so on.

Gaps are quite commonplace. The median number of gaps per day for the stocks that met our criteria was 31; on over one-half of the trading days, there were more than 31 gaps. The liquidity constraints were fairly rigorous, so there are actually many more stocks that gap on a typical day. Individual investors should not have difficulty finding potential gap-based trades.

Something that came as a surprise was that the number of gaps has been growing over time. There were more gaps (32,232) in 2011 than in any of the preceding 16 years. As shown in Table 3.1, the annual increase in the number of gaps has been quite steady.

Some days have an extremely high number of gaps. Refer to Table 3.2 to see the 25 days with the most gaps. The total number of gaps ranges from 553 to 1,277. Another remarkable thing about 2011 shows up in this table; 9 of the 10 days with the highest number of gaps occurred in 2011. One gap direction was always dominant. The highest number of gaps in the opposite direction from the majority was only 9; in 8 of the top 25 days, the gaps were entirely either up or down with none in the opposite direction.

There seems to be some slight seasonality in the number of gaps. In the study, more gaps (10.26% of the total) occur in September than in any other month, whereas December is the lowest month for gaps (6.66% of the total). Over the course of a week, the number of gaps was quite even between Monday and Thursday. On Fridays there were slightly fewer gaps (about 18% of the total).

All gaps are not created equal; some are much bigger than others. You saw how the percentage size of a gap can be calculated, which gives a relative measure of the size of the gap. Stocks can't gap down lower than –100%, but there is theoretically no upper limit to the size of an up gap. The most extreme gaps in the sample were an up gap of 151% and a down gap of –89%.

In addition to certain days having a higher concentration of gaps, certain stocks and certain industries can have far more than the average number of gaps for their category. The ten stocks in the study that had the highest number of gaps had gap totals ranging from 330 to 573. The industry with the highest number of total gaps was the semiconductor industry, which had a significantly larger number of gaps than its two closest competitors: exploration and production, and oil equipment and services. Approximately 31% of the total number of gaps fell into one of the ten industries shown in Table 3.8.

In the research, no foolproof get-rich methods for trading gaps were found. However, knowing some of the tendencies can be useful in trading. In subsequent chapters gaps will be dissected at deeper levels. There are some clues as to where you might focus your attention for gap trading.

Endnotes

1. The authors originally considered gaps going back to 1950 and found an increasing incidence of gaps in recent years, which raised questions about the benefits of going further back in time in the analysis. The 1995–2011 period provides enough market diversity to analyze both bear and bull markets while minimizing some of the problems, such as how to control for market returns and liquidity measures, which occur when trying to analyze data from several decades ago.

2. Issues such as stock splits add complications to determining historical liquidity measures for stocks. Suppose a stock trades for $6 a share and has a volume of 1 million shares on Monday; this company's dollar volume of trading would be $6 million. If the stock splits on Tuesday and the volume on Tuesday is 2 million shares at a price of $3, the dollar trading volume would be $6 million. The historical price is adjusted to $3 so that it does not appear that the

company's stock just lost half its value. However, historical volume is reported as the actual volume. So, going back and looking at the dollar volume on Monday, it would appear to be only $3 X 1 million shares or $3 million. Therefore, you need to use a lower dollar volume to filter for liquidity constraints in earlier years.

3. Interestingly, September 17 doesn't make the list of the top 25 highest gap days. The market did experience a large decline, however, with the DJIA falling 7.1%. The 684 point loss was the biggest-ever one-day point decline the market had experienced until September 29, 2008 when it declined 777 points.

Chapter 4

How to Measure Returns

How do you tell whether a given investment strategy is worth following? Although this seems like a simple question, it isn't. Suppose your friend Daniel tells you that he has developed an incredible trading strategy. He tells you that he made a 20% return on ABC, a 25% return on DEF, and a 35% return on GHI over the past month! Daniel offers to share his strategy with you so that you, too, may enjoy these gains. Daniel's returns do sound impressive, but, unfortunately, it isn't that simple. As we look at how we measure returns, we must also consider two other important factors: luck and risk.

Calculating Returns

With this discussion as backdrop, let's now turn to how we measure the profitability of gap-based trades in this book. Chapter 1, "What Are Gaps?" discussed how to number the days around gaps. The day of the gap is called Day 0. The day before is Day –1, the day after is

Day 1, and so forth. Because a gap can't be unambiguously determined until the close of Day 0, there would be no opportunity to initiate a gap-based trade until Day 1. Of course, there would be some days for which you could safely guess by the last hour or last minutes of trading that either a down gap or an up gap was going to occur. But, the Flash Crash of May 6, 2010, showed that prices can change quickly and dramatically.

Assuming that gap-based trades are initiated at the open of Day 1, we performed calculations using various holding periods. The formula used for the return based on a holding period of N days follows:

$$\text{N-Day Return} = \frac{(\text{Close Day N} - \text{Open Day 1})}{(\text{Open Day 1})}$$

This book reports results for holding periods of 1, 3, 5, 10, and 30 days. As an illustration, consider Figure 4.1 which shows a gap up for KO on March 24, 2011. March 24 is labeled as Day 0. Seeing that a gap up occurred on March 24, you can enter a long position at the open the following day. Thus, you can purchase KO on Day 1 at a price of $64.87. The closing price for KO on Day 1 is $65.22. Hence, your 1-day return follows:

$$\text{1-Day Return} = \frac{(65.22 - 64.87)}{(64.87)} = 0.0054$$

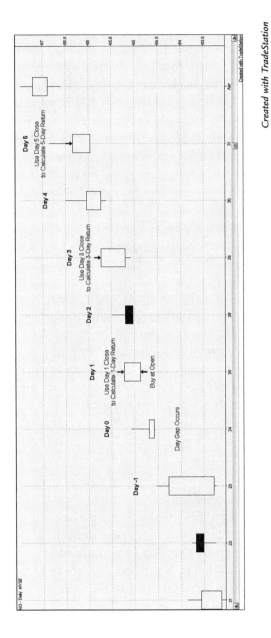

FIGURE 4.1   *Daily stock chart for KO, March 21–April 1, 2011*

The 1-day return is simply measuring how much you would earn if you bought the stock at the open on Day 1 and sold at the close on Day 1. You can calculate longer returns in the same manner. For example, a 3-day return is calculated assuming that KO is purchased at the open of Day 1 and sold at the close of Day 3. The closing price on Day 3, March 29, was 65.72 leading to a 3-day return of 0.0131, calculated as follows:

$$3\text{-Day Return} = \frac{(65.72 - 64.87)}{64.87} = 0.0131$$

In the same manner, the 5-day return follows:

$$5\text{-Day Return} = \frac{(66.34 - 64.87)}{64.87} = 0.0227$$

These calculations do not make any adjustments for transactions costs. The profit that an investor would actually make on this trade would be reduced by the costs, such as commissions, the investor must pay to enter the trades. In recent years, transactions costs have fallen dramatically. Also, transactions costs vary widely across investors, depending upon their portfolios and trading frequency. Therefore, returns not adjusted for transactions are reported, allowing individual investors to determine if the profitability of a strategy would be great enough to cover their transactions costs.

Table 4.1 provides the average returns for stocks that gapped during the 1995–2011 sample period. All these returns are calculated for long positions; if a stock gapped up or down on Day 0, a long position is entered at the open on Day 1. The returns shown are in percentages. So, the value of –0.0204 for the average 1-day return for down gap stocks means –0.0204%. Likewise, the 5-day return from buying stocks that experienced down gaps was 0.3712%, or a little more than 1/3 of 1%. Another way to state this is in basis points. One basis point (abbreviated bp) is 1/100th of 1%; 100 bp equals 1%. The return of 0.3712% could be described as 37.12 bp. These numbers sound quite small. However, 37.12 bp over a 5-day period is approximately 20.35% on an annualized basis (assuming about 250 trading days in a year).

TABLE 4.1   *Average Returns for Stocks with Gaps, 1995–2011*

	Average Gap Size	Number of Occurrences	Returns				
			1-day	3-day	5-day	10-day	30-day
All Down Gaps	-1.3394	97,029	-0.0204	0.0198	0.3712	0.4793	1.3558
All Up Gaps	1.1052	116,903	-0.0903	-0.1802	-0.0229	-0.0474	0.9449

Now look more closely at the returns for stocks that gap down. On average, the 1-day return for these stocks is negative. Thus, on average, after a stock gaps down, the stock price continues to fall over the next day. Entering a long position on Day 1 after a stock experiences a down gap on Day 0 results, on average, in a loss the first day. By Day 3, however, the price movement has reversed, resulting in positive returns for the 3-day, 5-day, 10-day, and 30-day holding periods.

Now, consider the returns for stocks that gap up. The numbers in Table 4.1 show that, on average, the stock price is lower at the close on Day 1, Day 3, Day 5, and Day 10 than it was at the open of Day 1. Thus, the upward movement in price seen on the day of the gap does not continue over the next couple of weeks. Entering a long position on Day 1 for these stocks would be unprofitable over the next 10 days. You do see, however, positive returns for long positions held for 30 days.

These returns suggest that going long, hoping for a continuation of price movement, the day after an up gap, is not immediately profitable. For holding periods of 10 days or less, a better strategy would be to short a stock after an up gap. Up gaps appear to be associated with a reversal in price trend over the short (10-day) time frame. Down gaps do appear to be associated with price continuation, that is, the price continues downward, for a short period of time, suggesting a short position is initially profitable. Within 3 days, however, this price movement tends to reverse, suggesting that a long position should follow a down gap for holding periods of 3 days or longer.

Daily and Annualized Returns

The authors report nominal returns for the various time periods. These returns are not, except for the case of 1-day returns, daily returns, nor are they annualized returns. Consider, for example, the 5-day return of 0.3712 and the 10-day return of 0.4793 for down gaps in Table 4.1. These numbers are not directly comparable; in other words you cannot simply say that the 10-day return is better because it is a bigger number. How would you convert these returns to annualized returns? The 5-day return says that over a 5-day time period you would have earned 0.3712%; there are 50 5-day time periods in a year (assuming 250 trading days). Thus, with compounding, an annualized return would be $(1 + 0.003712)^{50} - 1 = 20.35\%$. The 10-day return of 0.4793 would be $(1 + 0.004793)^{25} - 1 = 12.70\%$.

You must also be careful about how to view price movement. Consider, for example, the 1-day, 3-day, and 5-day returns for up gaps in Table 4.1. If, after an up gap, an investor purchased the stock at the open on Day 1 and sold it at the close on that day, the investor would, on average, have a loss of 0.09%. If an investor bought at the open on Day 1 and sold at the close on Day 3, the loss would be 0.18%. Thus, price must have moved lower between the close on Day 1 and the close on Day 3. If an investor bought at the open on Day 1 and sold at the close on Day 5, the loss would be only 0.02%. Although the 5-day return is still negative, it is smaller in absolute value than the 3-day return; thus, the price must have moved higher between the close on Day 3 and the close on Day 5. However, the upward price movement was not enough to overcome the downward movement of the first 3 days.

The Impact of Luck

The authors live in San Antonio, home of the Alamodome, which was primarily designed as a football stadium even though San Antonio has no pro football team. Go figure. Let's conduct a thought experiment. There is a football game and the Alamodome, which can hold approximately 80,000 people, is packed. At halftime you hold a special coin-flipping event. You have everyone stand up and flip a coin. You tell everyone who flipped "tails" to sit down. You then tell the people still standing to repeat this process. You continue this process until only one person, the champion head-flipper, remains. If the coins were all fair coins, you would expect the sequence of people still standing to be something like 40,000, 20,000, 10,000, 5,000, and so on. It is quite likely that the winner, whom you can call Pat, might have flipped 16 or more consecutive heads.[1]

A reporter might interview Pat about her head-flipping success. The interview might begin with the reporter asking, "Pat, tell me. Were you surprised when you flipped 16 consecutive heads in a row?"

Would you expect Pat's response to be, "No, not really. You see when I was in college, I skipped a lot of my classes. I spent hours practicing coin flipping. Somehow I knew that someday it would pay off. Today it has. I get to be on national TV. Hi, Mom! I told you it would all work out someday."

Or do you think a response such as, "I'm as surprised as you are. I guess today was my lucky day. It was definitely blind luck, but it will certainly make a good story for my grandkids." would be more likely?

So what does this have to do with investing? Given thousands and thousands of investors, some people are bound to get lucky. Just as you need to question whether a winning coin flipper has some special talent or simply got lucky, you must ask whether an investor's winning record is a result of a superior investment strategy or simply luck. Was Daniel in the opening scenario of this chapter like Pat? Did his investment strategy win just due to pure luck?

Be careful not to attribute good performance and a high return to a superior trading methodology too quickly. As you have just seen, you can win repeatedly just because of luck. As American screenwriter Frank Howard Clark said, "It's hard to detect good luck—it looks so much like something you've earned." Knowing when to attribute good performance to luck and when to attribute it to methodology is a difficult task. One way to do this is to see if the strategy makes rational sense. If Pat were to tell you that the winning methodology for coin flipping was to stand on her left foot when she tossed the coin, you would attribute her winning to luck. Likewise, if Daniel's stock-picking methodology were to pick stocks by choosing three stock tickers by pulling tickers from a hat that contained slips of papers with the names of all the tickers in the S&P500, you would attribute his performance to luck. But, sometimes, it isn't easy to tell if the strategy makes rational sense. Suppose that Daniel said he picked stocks based on a recent vacation he took to a west coast city. He saw lots of new businesses opening, a booming real estate market, and a vibrant economy. He enjoyed his visit so much he decided to invest in companies headquartered in that city. Was Daniel's good performance luck? Or did Daniel's strategy help him choose companies that were growing and in an expanding industry?

In addition to asking whether rational reasons exist for a winning strategy, you can control for risk to some degree by using large sample sizes. Pat may throw 16 heads in a row, but can she throw 20 heads in row by standing on her left foot? What about 25 or 30 heads? As you increase the sample size and the time period considered, the chance to have a winning strategy simply because of luck diminishes.

The Impact of Risk

The second factor with which you need to wrestle is risk. Say someone comes to you with a stock-picking system that produces a high number of winning trades.

The relevant risk question is, "Does this system merely tend to select stocks with high risk?" If so, the results may not look so impressive after adjusting for risk.

But, how do you adjust for risk? There's the rub. One method frequently used in academic finance is to adjust based on the stock's beta, which is a measure of the stock's systematic, or nondiversifiable, risk. This is part of what is called Modern Portfolio Theory (MPT). The work that went into MPT led to Nobel Prizes for Harry Markowitz and William Sharpe in 1990.

Although beta is commonly used as a measure of risk in the academic world, it is not without problems. Academics are still arguing about risk adjustments. The last doctoral dissertation on risk and asset pricing has not yet been written and probably won't be for many years (if ever). For the most part, academics identify risk as uncertainty or variability of returns. This concept isn't perfectly transferable into the practitioners world of trading.

First, practitioners are not so concerned that a trade might be more profitable than what they expected. For example, if a trader thinks there is a 95% chance that a trade will make $100,000 and a 5% chance that the trade will make $1 million, risk would not be much of a concern for the practitioner. Give the same trader a trade that had a 95% chance of making $100,000 and a 5% chance of losing $800,000, however, and risk becomes much more of a concern. To the academic, both of these trades have about the same variability and, thus, about the same risk. Academics don't distinguish much between upside risk and downside risk; the unknown, or variability, is risk. For the trader, the possibility of loss is a much greater risk than the possibility of an extremely high gain.

Second, academics have focused on how diversification minimizes risk by eliminating unsystematic risk. Although it is true that diversification curbs huge losses by spreading your eggs across a number of different baskets, it does nothing, as the last decade has taught us, to protect investors when the entire market is in a downturn.

Practitioners generally define risk as the chance of losing capital. This can be an entirely different mindset than the academic view of risk. A number of alternative measures have been put forth to try to address the notion of risk in a trading environment. These include measures such as maximum amount of loss per trade and maximum drawdown. None of the measures developed so far perfectly meet the needs of all traders.

Obviously, measures of risk are complicated and controversial. Thus, throughout this book, the only adjustments made are controlling for overall market conditions. Individual traders need to be aware of what measures of risk are most appropriate given their own definition of risk.

Why adjust for overall market conditions? Remember Daniel from the beginning of the chapter? He made 20% in ABC, 25%, and DEF, and 35% in GHI last month. When analyzing Daniel's strategy, economists will be quick to ask, "What was the opportunity cost?" In other words, if Daniel had placed his money in another stock, what would his return have been? If the average stock in the market went up 35% last month, Daniel's strategy doesn't look so good any more. His GHI pick was simply an "average" pick.

Even though he made a positive return in ABC and DEF, he would have made more money purchasing the average stock in the market.

Therefore, you need to consider the overall background of the market when considering how well an investment does. You don't want to brag about a 25% return when the average return is 35%; in this case, you did 10% worse than if you just randomly picked stocks. Under some market conditions, it is just easier to make money in the stock market than it is during other time periods. Having a 25% return during a strong market uptrend is much easier than having a 25% return when the market is in a sideways trading range.

Market Adjusted Returns

How can you control for market conditions? You do so by calculating market-adjusted returns. As most things in investments, this adjustment is not as straightforward as it sounds. As a measure of underlying market conditions, you can use the S&P500 as your adjustment. Trading in SPY, an ETF that tracks the S&P500, began in 1993, which enables you to use SPY returns for adjustment as follows.

N-day market-adjusted return = N-day return – N-day return for SPY

This adjustment is not perfect. Theoretically, you want to adjust the return for your strategy by the return you would have received if you invested in the average stock that has the same risk. We screened companies using minimum volume and minimum dollar volume criteria (as described in Chapter 3, "The Occurrence of Gaps") to avoid thinly traded, illiquid stocks. Although we removed extremely small and illiquid companies from the sample, stocks that have a smaller market capitalization than the stocks in the S&P Small-Cap 600 remain in the sample. Thus, the sample contains stocks with a wide range of market capitalizations. Academics will be quick to point out that the risk metrics of a pool of stocks with such a wide range of market capitalization are not identical to those of SPY; thus, the adjustment made in this book for market returns is not perfect.

Use extra care when interpreting market-adjusted returns during a market downturn. The market-adjusted return is an attempt to tell how much better a strategy did than investing in stocks randomly does. If the market falls 20% and you follow a strategy that loses 5%, you have outperformed the market. Your market adjusted return would by –5% – (–20%) or 15%! Of course, an investor would rather lose 5% than 20%, but a 5% loss is a negative return. Don't get misled by positive market-adjusted returns in a market downturn; any negative returns result in a loss of capital, something you want to avoid.

These issues are mentioned in the interest of full disclosure. The market return adjustment made in this study was simple and has its problems, but it does provide some additional, useful information.

Table 4.2 shows the market-adjusted returns for the data presented in Table 4.1. Although the 1-day return for down gaps was –0.0204, the market-adjusted 1-day return is –0.0507. That the market-adjusted return is lower than the nonadjusted return indicates the overall market was moving higher the day after the down gap. Thus, purchasing the stock that down gapped not only resulted in a negative 1-day return, but it also meant an opportunity cost of not receiving the positive return that would have resulted if that money had been invested in the market portfolio.

One important result in Table 4.2 is that, even though the average 3-day return for stocks that gap down is positive, the market-adjusted 3-day return for these stocks is negative. This means that purchasing a stock that gaps down at the open on Day 1 and holding it for 3 days, on average, results in a profit, but the profit is smaller than what would have been earned if you had invested in the market portfolio.

The numbers presented in Table 4.2 are averages of many observations over a 17-year time frame. The overall market conditions in the late 1990s were radically different than they have been since the turn of the century. Chapter 3 noted that gaps had become more common in recent years. This leads to the question of whether the averaging of so much data in Table 4.2 masks some underlying, important trends. To better understand how stable these results have been over time, the returns are broken down by year. Table 4.3 presents returns for down gaps by year from 1995 through 2011. Negative numbers are lightly shaded to discern patterns more easily.

TABLE 4.2 *Average Market-Adjusted Returns for Stocks with Gaps, 1995–2011*

	Gap Size	Number of Occurrences	Returns					Market-Adjusted Returns				
			1-day	3-day	5-day	10-day	30-day	1-day	3-day	5-day	10-day	30-day
All Down Gaps	-1.3394	97,029	-0.0204	0.0198	0.3712	0.4793	1.3558	-0.0507	-0.0013	0.0478	0.1116	0.3783
All Up Gaps	1.1052	116,903	-0.0903	-0.1802	-0.0229	-0.0474	0.9449	-0.0588	-0.1110	-0.0337	-0.0483	0.3631

TABLE 4.3 *Returns for Down Gaps by Year, 1995–2011*

Year	Gap Size	Number of Occurrences	Returns					Market-Adjusted Returns				
			1-day	3-day	5-day	10-day	30-day	1-day	3-day	5-day	10-day	30-day
1995	-1.3023	1,274	0.3172	0.7493	0.8964	1.2647	2.2550	0.1313	0.3366	0.2599	-0.0848	-1.1956
1996	-1.1777	1,777	-0.0556	0.0736	0.3934	1.2308	3.2126	0.0639	0.1649	0.3175	0.4494	0.6175
1997	-1.1929	2,237	0.1855	0.0989	0.2848	0.4429	1.9616	-0.0433	-0.1393	-0.1887	-0.6442	-1.8903
1998	-1.4255	3,219	-0.0091	-0.1638	0.2016	0.8749	2.5654	-0.0706	-0.2794	-0.3362	-0.1981	-0.6552
1999	-1.6586	2,863	0.0082	0.4815	0.7240	0.7223	2.9440	0.2137	0.4827	0.5501	0.2234	1.1633
2000	-2.1548	4,024	0.0360	0.4650	0.4580	0.6362	0.3275	0.0679	0.1088	0.2870	0.1957	0.3811
2001	-1.7198	4,907	-0.0623	-0.9270	-0.4157	0.0215	-0.8005	-0.1408	-0.5437	-0.2388	-0.0340	0.1537
2002	-1.4916	4,936	0.0129	-0.3626	-0.5783	-1.0941	-1.7706	-0.0708	-0.0495	0.0087	0.0129	0.3132
2003	-1.2004	3,978	0.1334	0.5145	0.8391	1.9453	5.7533	0.0778	0.3938	0.5013	0.9554	2.5535
2004	-1.2986	5,186	-0.0748	0.0540	0.0985	0.8380	2.0080	0.0056	-0.0418	-0.0886	0.2880	0.6813
2005	-1.2459	5,072	0.0103	0.2252	0.3589	0.5637	2.0576	0.0221	0.1142	0.1434	0.1984	0.9452
2006	-1.2274	6,308	0.0003	-0.1314	-0.0051	0.3160	1.3133	-0.0421	-0.1496	-0.1828	-0.1476	-0.1071
2007	-1.2039	7,578	-0.0501	-0.2890	-0.1865	-0.6698	-0.2041	-0.0712	-0.1121	-0.2278	-0.4864	-0.5195
2008	-1.6215	9,244	-0.5673	-1.7933	-0.6252	-2.1224	-6.1998	-0.3644	-0.3062	-0.1950	-0.2002	-0.7227
2009	-1.3705	8,360	-0.1595	0.5980	1.2581	1.9083	8.8321	-0.0430	0.1955	0.5622	0.8984	3.8003
2010	-0.9937	9,973	0.0348	-0.0202	0.7781	1.1395	3.1656	-0.0382	-0.0123	0.1839	0.4180	0.9523
2011	-1.1607	16,093	0.2373	0.9669	1.0655	1.2432	0.9119	-0.0161	0.1640	-0.0292	-0.0383	-0.7551
All Down Gaps	-1.3394	97,029	-0.0204	0.0198	0.3712	0.4793	1.3558	-0.0507	-0.0013	0.0478	0.1116	0.3783

The results in Table 4.3 highlight some of the differences in considering nominal returns versus considering market-adjusted returns. Look at 1997. The nominal returns for purchasing a stock at the open the day after it gaps are positive for all the holding periods, yet the market-adjusted returns for all holding periods are negative. The market, as measured by the S&P500, rose by 33.36% in 1997. Although the prices of stocks that gapped down reversed by the next day, they tended not to rise as much as other stocks over the next 30 trading days. A similar result occurred in 2011. In 2011, the S&P500 rose only 2.05%, so a bull market cannot be the explanation for the negative market-adjusted returns. As you can see when you look at market conditions more closely in Chapter 8, "Gaps and the Market," 2011 was characterized by some extreme price moves within a trading range without much directional movement. Interestingly, although the size has changed, the 1-day market-adjusted return for down gaps has been negative each of the last 6 years.

The results for up gaps are broken down by year in Table 4.4. The nominal returns for all holding periods were negative for four of the years: 2002, 2007, 2008, and 2011. The market-adjusted returns for all holding periods were negative for 5 years: 1995, 1996, 2006, 2007, and 2011. The nominal returns for all holding periods were positive for three of the years: 1995, 2009, and 2010; the only year in which the market-adjusted returns were all positive was 2009.

TABLE 4.4   Returns for Up Gaps by Year, 1995–2011

Year	Gap Size	Number of Occurrences	Returns					Market-Adjusted Returns				
			1-day	3-day	5-day	10-day	30-day	1-day	3-day	5-day	10-day	30-day
1995	0.8952	1,772	0.0347	0.0181	0.1235	0.3674	2.9599	-0.0225	-0.2434	-0.3374	-0.5433	-0.1907
1996	0.9418	2,260	-0.0383	-0.1807	-0.1126	0.2148	1.9931	-0.0932	-0.3568	-0.3708	-0.4860	-0.5231
1997	0.9654	3,335	-0.1029	0.0596	0.1078	0.4828	1.7833	-0.0485	0.0043	-0.1016	-0.3489	-0.6750
1998	1.1555	4,026	-0.0993	0.2625	0.4964	1.2869	3.9484	-0.1844	-0.1312	-0.0774	-0.0148	0.2018
1999	1.3209	4,452	-0.2067	-0.0685	0.0795	1.2123	3.8325	-0.1775	-0.0431	-0.0246	0.7317	2.7696
2000	1.6444	4,933	-0.3499	-0.3968	-0.6840	-1.1378	0.4495	-0.1787	-0.1011	-0.1953	-0.3494	1.1358
2001	1.2807	4,970	0.2445	-0.3378	-0.0520	0.3235	-0.1705	0.0996	-0.2266	0.0145	0.3257	0.5058
2002	1.1821	5,390	-0.1293	-0.2708	-0.3334	-0.7834	-1.2608	-0.2153	-0.0777	0.1572	0.1461	0.5855
2003	0.9670	6,344	-0.1069	0.3277	0.4856	0.8994	4.6193	-0.0816	0.0413	0.1531	0.3347	1.4949
2004	0.9917	6,300	0.0297	-0.0316	0.2785	0.1979	0.8548	-0.091	-0.1658	0.0483	-0.0467	0.3055
2005	1.0254	7,117	-0.2096	-0.1866	-0.1850	0.1810	1.7276	-0.1456	-0.2257	-0.2381	-0.1009	0.8938
2006	1.0513	8,659	-0.0969	-0.1571	-0.1006	-0.0452	0.3952	-0.0895	-0.2212	-0.1438	-0.1642	-0.6359
2007	1.0819	9,862	-0.1358	-0.2932	-0.4613	-0.6511	-1.3642	-0.0487	-0.1757	-0.2160	-0.2973	-0.4516
2008	1.4899	7,662	-0.6464	-0.7273	-1.2769	-2.7920	-6.2900	0.0427	0.1832	0.0291	-0.3041	-0.2597
2009	1.2478	10,719	0.3161	0.3441	1.5496	2.1140	5.1956	0.1683	0.1200	0.5958	0.8311	2.0278
2010	0.8404	12,963	0.1944	0.0852	0.3337	0.4016	2.8071	0.0109	-0.0523	0.0190	0.0522	0.7920
2011	0.9759	16,139	-0.2761	-0.7475	-0.5686	-1.1488	-0.8432	-0.1407	-0.3079	-0.2948	-0.6390	-0.9923
All Up Gaps	1.1052	116,903	-0.0903	-0.1802	-0.0229	-0.0474	0.9449	-0.0588	-0.1110	-0.0337	-0.0483	0.3631

The up gap results for 1995 are particularly striking; all the nominal results are positive, but all the market-adjusted returns for that year were negative. The average 30-day nominal return for purchasing a stock on the day after it gapped up was 2.9599, which is about 27.52% on an annualized basis. However, the S&P500 gained 37.8% in 1995. Thus, even though stocks that gapped up saw continuation in upward price movement, they did not rally as much as the broader market. When the gains earned from investing in the stocks that gapped up are compared to the opportunity cost of not being invested in the broader market in 1995, the market-adjusted returns are negative.

Another year that is particularly interesting is 2009 in which nominal returns and market-adjusted returns were all positive. The nominal returns in 2009 were remarkably high. The 5-day return of 1.5496 translated into an annualized rate of 115.73%. The 10-day return of 2.114 is equivalent to an annualized rate of 68.7%; the 30-day return of 2.8071 is an annualized rate of 52.51%. Investors purchasing a broad portfolio of stocks, as measured by the S&P500, earned 26.46% that year. Thus, a portion of the profits earned by an investor purchasing stocks after they gapped up were attributed to the bull market, but this accounted for only about half of the profits. It appears that gap ups signaled which stocks would outperform the market in 2009. Although not as strong, you can see similar results for 2010.

Extreme Values

Extreme values in any set of data are always interesting. From an investing standpoint the extreme values are especially intriguing. What trades would have been the most profitable? What trades would have been the least profitable? Would it reasonably have been possible to spot these opportunities beforehand? What can be learned for future reference?

The extreme cases presented in this chapter are from 2011. This is done for a couple of reasons. First, it is the last year in the sample and therefore is of particular interest as the most current year in the study. Second, in Chapter 3 you saw that the frequency of gaps has been increasing over the years; in Table 3.1 you saw that with 32,232 gaps, 2011 had more than any other year in the sample. With that many gaps, surely some interesting extreme examples exist.

First, consider the stocks that were extreme in terms of the number of gaps. Two stocks tied for the highest number of down gaps in 2011; both Resmed Inc. (RMD) and Unisys Corp. (UIS) had 25 down gaps in 2011. With approximately 250 trading days in a year, that means that RMD and UIS were experiencing a down gap on about 10% of the trading days. RMD, shown in Figure 4.2, makes medical equipment related to respiratory ailments. UIS, shown in Figure 4.3, is an information technology company. The company with the highest number of up gaps was Apple Inc (AAPL) with 24; the stock chart of AAPL is shown in Figure 4.4. All three of these companies have strong links to technology. Because technology stocks tend to be volatile, it is not surprising that these stocks top the list for the highest number of gaps.

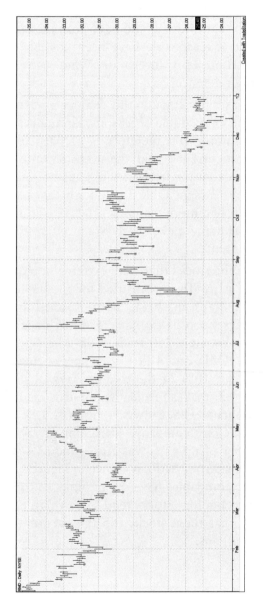

FIGURE 4.2   Daily stock chart for RMD, January 1–December 31, 2011

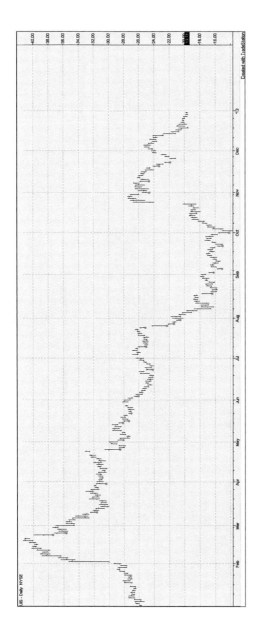

FIGURE 4.3 *Daily stock chart for UIS, January 1–December 31, 2011*

Created with TradeStation

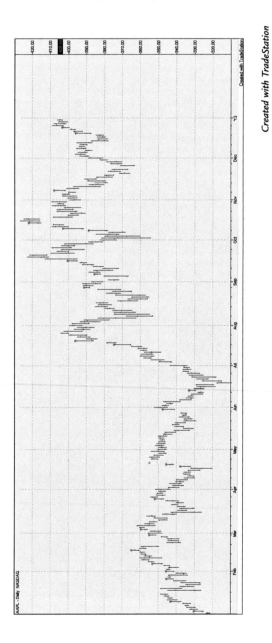

FIGURE 4.4   Daily stock chart for AAPL, January 1—December 31, 2011

Stock charts for the three stocks share some similarities but are quite different. The high number of gaps makes all three charts look somewhat choppy. The chart for RMD is especially irregular. The gaps create several large gaps in price. Overall, the stock trended down in price over the year, falling almost 30%, but did so in fits and starts. Although RMD experienced at least one gap down every month in 2011, the stock experienced an unusually high number of down gaps in September. In the first 15 trading days of September, RMD had five down gaps. Surprisingly, the stock also had two up gaps during that same 15-day period. Thus, for the first 3 weeks in September, RMD experienced a gap almost every other day.

Looking at UIS in Figure 4.3, you see that the stock increased approximately 40% from the beginning of 2011 through mid-February. During this rapid increase, the stock experienced no down gaps. However, the story quickly changed on March 22 when a down gap, followed by a down gap on March 23, caused the price of UIS to fall by more than 12%. For the rest of the year, UIS trended downward. Five down gaps occurred during July, with the last five trading days of July seeing four down gaps. During October, the stock experienced a short uptrend, during which no down gaps occurred. Just as in February, however, this uptrend came to a halt with a down gap on the first trading day in November. The stock price continued to fall, losing approximately 20% over the November–December time frame. Thus, for UIS, down gaps were associated with the time frames that UIS was in a downward trend.

In Figure 4.4, you can see that AAPL was in a trading range for the first half of 2011, In July, AAPL experienced an uptrend; by September, the stock was again in a trading range. For the most part, the up gaps for AAPL were spread across the year. No more gaps occurred during the uptrend than during trading ranges. Most noticeable, AAPL did experience three up gaps in a row in late April. However, these up gaps were not enough to push the stock out of the trading range.

Profitable Trading Examples

Now consider some particular gap trades that would have been highly profitable. In particular, which trades were the best trades in 2011? The single best 10-day trade after a down gap would have been to buy Clearwire Corporation (CLWR) after its August 8 down gap. Clearwire is an interesting company. It has a 4G mobile broadband network that extends across much of the United States and reaches about one-third of the U.S. population. Its service is branded CLEAR in most of its markets. CLWR went public with its March 2007 IPO at a price of $25. By the end of 2008, the price was hovering around $4. In September 2009, its price recovered to more than $9. For the next year CLWR traded in a $6–8 range. In October 2010, the price began a steady descent from about $8, dipping below $2 for the first time in August 2011. As shown in Figure 4.5, on August 8, 2011, the stock gapped down closing at $1.52. However, there was a dramatic turnaround at that point. The 10-day return from the open on August 9 was an amazing 94%.

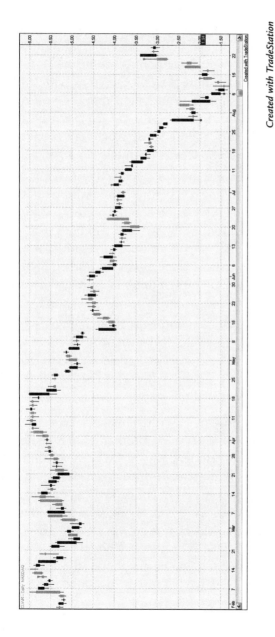

FIGURE 4.5   *Stock chart for CLWR, January 31—August 24, 2011*

Created with TradeStation

Hindsight is always 20/20. Now it is easy to identify the August 8 down gap as an exhaustion gap. But, were there clues that might have pointed someone to a buy decision around that time period? The stock had gapped down three times in the preceding 3 months—on April 27, May 12, and July 28. In the 25 trading days between July 5 and August 8, the stock had black candles on all but 5 days. It was definitely on a bad roll.

What was happening with CLWR? Revenue had gone from $20 million in 2008 to $557 million in 2010. In 2011, the company was on a path to push revenue to more than $1 billion. However, the company was still incurring dramatic losses. The company had been making large investments in plant, property, and equipment. It also had more than $800 million in cash at the end of June.

At the time, the company was receiving some mention in the press due to Raj Rajaratnam's insider trading trial. On May 11, a *Forbes* article titled "I Knew Rajaratnam Was a Crook After He Tried to Sell Me Insider Info" contained this paragraph:

> Clearwire (CLWR) was often mentioned in the reporting on this trial as another entity about which Intel's investment was made known to Raj before it was made known to the general public. The Clearwire connection concerned the building of a nationwide Wi-Fi network which at this moment remains the fastest network extant. Even if you own a new 4G phone (I bought one last week), they will tell you in the phone store to use Wi-Fi if it is available because it is so much faster than any cellular connection.[2]

The company was getting attention for its fast Wi-Fi network but in the context of an insider trading trial. The former was clearly good press. However, the latter was not. No company, regardless of the facts of the case, wants to be mentioned in connection with insider trading. This may have been an additional factor dragging the stock price down. On May 12, the company's stock dropped by 15.6%.

Could astute investors have put all this information together and bought at the open on August 9? If they had done that, they might not have kept their position through the day. It opened at 1.56, reached a high of 1.62, hit a low of 1.35, and closed at 1.42. The trade might have been stopped out. The stock was also quite volatile on the 10th, with a range from 1.32 to 1.68, closing at 1.44. But, here's where things get more interesting. On the 11th the stock closed at 1.59. On the 12th it gapped up, closing at 1.91. With its second up gap in 4 days on the 17th, it closed at 2.33. Two days later it gapped up again and closed at 3.01. Even if investors had waited to buy until after the 2nd gap up during this period, they could have caught the move from the open on the 18th at 2.21 to the close on the 19th at 3.01; that would have been a 36% gain.

Buying on the 9th would have been betting on a reversal. Going long after observing a gap up on either August 12 or August 17 would have been pursuing a continuation strategy. So how do you reconcile this with the observation that a reversal approach generally seems to be more profitable? This book is about trading gaps. Although the authors present evidence that points toward the advantage of a reversal approach in general, it isn't appropriate in every case. In this particular case

CLWR had continued its downward march after the three down gaps on April 27, May 12, and July 28. It also closed down on the August 10 after the down gap on the 8th. After the up gap on the August 12, the price went up. There was certainly a case to be made to use a continuation approach on either August 12 or the August 17. If you throw in the other factors (rapidly rising revenue, building a leading edge network, lots of cash on the balance sheet, and some unfortunate linkage to an insider trading case), there were some good reasons to suspect that perhaps it was about time for the 4-month march from $6 to $2 to reverse course. There was even one more factor; on August 10 the company announced that the chief operating officer was promoted to president and CEO and that the company's chairman and interim CEO was becoming the executive chairman of the board of directors. There were some important changes occurring.

Trading the August 18 down gap for Universal Display Corporation (PANL) had the highest 5-day return for any down gap in 2011. PANL engages in the research, development, and commercialization of OLED technologies and materials for use in flat panel display. Figure 4.6 illustrates the price movement of PANL from December 2010 through September 2011. Over a 4-month time period, December 2010 through March 2011, PANL doubled in price. Following this 4-month uptrend, a 4-month downtrend ensued. This downtrend was just as strong as the uptrend, and PANL lost more than half of its value. On August 8, PANL closed below $25 per share, ending the downtrend. By August 15, PANL had reached $36, representing more than a 40% gain over a 1-week time period. This price increase appeared to be fueled by better than expected sales and profit numbers. However, the enthusiasm was short-lived, within 3 days PANL dropped back down below $28 a share. At the time, someone watching the stock and seeing the down gap on August 18 would have easily thought that PANL was still in a downtrend. In hindsight, that down gap was a great buying opportunity. Enthusiasm for PANL quickly returned as a licensing agreement with Samsung was announced on August 23. Buying PANL at the open on August 19, the day following the gap, and holding the stock for 5 days would have resulted in a 69.5% return; holding the stock for 10 days would have resulted in a 77.7% return.

Interestingly, PANL also had a down gap on March 14, 2011, which also was followed by a high rate of return over the next several weeks. The March 15 down gap broke through a significant trend line, suggesting an end to the uptrend. However, the following day, PANL gapped up and continued in an even steeper uptrend. Thus, both of these profitable trading opportunities were a result of a down gap, which at the time suggested a change in trend, but in hindsight were a fabulous buying opportunity.

You looked at several of the most profitable opportunities for going long after a down gap in 2011. These were basically opportunities in which the down gap price movement quickly reversed after the down gap. Now consider some of the most profitable trading opportunities with up gaps.

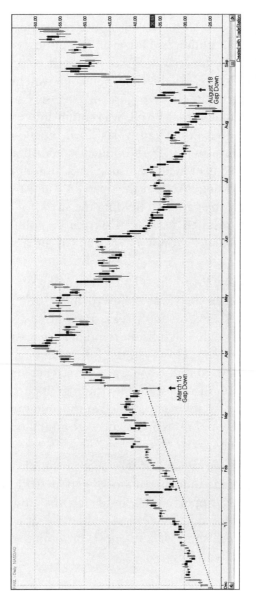

FIGURE 4.6   *Daily stock chart for PANL, December 1, 2010—September 20, 2011*

On October 17, 2011, Cheniere Energy Inc. (LNG) experienced a gap up. An investor who purchased LNG the following day would have made a 91.6% gain in 10 days. LNG builds and operates liquefied natural gas terminals and pipelines. As Figure 4.7 shows, the October 17 gap was not spectacular, and nothing much happened to the stock price over the next week. The story changed, however, on October 26, when the stock gapped up again, this time in a spectacular move. The market stock price opened approximately 75% higher, and even though it moved down somewhat during the day, a gap of more than $2 a share remained. The price did continue to rise over the next few days, contributing to the 91.6% 10-day return, but the substantial price move on October 26 accounted for the majority of the gain. Why did the big price jump occur on October 26? LNG announced a major deal with a British energy firm to export liquefied natural gas out of the United States.

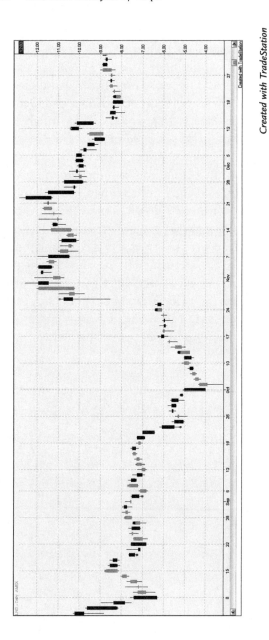

FIGURE 4.7   *Daily stock chart for LNG, August 3—December 31, 2011*

Created with TradeStation

Figure 4.8 contains a stock chart for Optimer Pharmaceutical, Inc. (OPTR). The stock entered an uptrend in mid-August. As this trend continued, an up gap occurred on September 7. Price continued to move up, resulting in a 21% 5-day return and a 53% 10-day return for investors who bought the stock at the open on September 8. From a technical standpoint, this is an interesting gap. Although many of the stocks that saw incredibly high returns after an up gap were buyout targets, OPTR does not fit into this category. There was an increasing interest in OPTR. The company appeared in a number of news reports for a variety of reasons. OPTR had recently had a drug receive FDA approval. The company was covered by new analysts. Several analysts increased their ratings of the company. These were all "positive" news stories, but there was not actually any new news about the company. As the uptrend continued, the company was included in lists of high-return companies. This is an example of the feedback loop about which technical analysts talk. As more people heard that others had made money in OPTR, more people began buying, driving the price up further. This increased interest in the stock shows up in rising volume throughout September. The September 7 gap can be viewed as a measuring gap, occurring about halfway up the price increase.

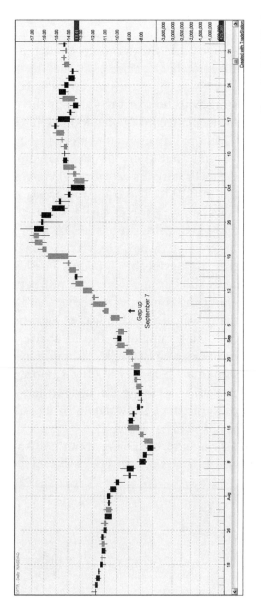

FIGURE 4.8   Daily stock chart for OPTR, August 12—November 1, 2011

Created with TradeStation

Summary

This chapter explained a methodology for calculating the returns for gap trading strategies. You saw that immediately after a gap occurs, whether it is a down gap or an up gap, price tends to move lower. These results hold whether looking at nominal returns or market-adjusted returns and suggest following a shorting strategy immediately after a gap. However, price movement quickly reverses, especially for gap down stocks, suggesting that a long strategy is more likely to be profitable over longer holding periods. As you continue through this book, you will look at how the consideration of additional variables, such as volume, price movement prior to the gap, and overall market measures, might increase the profitability of trading when a gap occurs.

Endnotes

1. The chance of flipping a head on a single coin toss is 1/2. The chance of flipping two heads in a row is 1/4; so out of four people, one person will, on average, flip two heads in a row.

2. Lapping, Joan. *I Knew Rajaratnam Was a Crook After He Tried to Sell Me Insider Information,*" Forbes Online, www.forbes.com/sites/joanlappin/2011/05/11/i-knew-rajaratnam-was-crooked-after-he-tried-to-sell-me-insider-info/.

Chapter 5

Gaps and Previous Price Movement

For a gap to occur, obviously there must be price movement from one day to the next. A gap up occurs when today's low is higher than yesterday's high. So on a gap up there had been an upward jump in price at the open. But what happened during the day of the gap? Did the stock close higher or lower than the open? If the closing price is higher than the opening price, you would chart it on a candlestick chart with a white candle body. If the close is lower than the open, the candle body is shaded black. This chapter examines the significance of the candle color on the day of the gap, which is referred to as Day 0, and the candle color the day before the gap, which is referred to as Day –1.

Chapter 2, "Windows on Candlestick Charts," focused on traditional candlestick patterns that contained gaps, or windows. These short-term patterns often considered the color of the candle on the day of the gap and the colors and positions of the candles 1 or 2 days after the gap. The analysis in this chapter is different in that the price movement leading up to the gap and on the day of the gap, rather than after the gap occurs, is examined.

Gap Day Candle Color

There are six basic gap day cases to consider—three down gap possibilities and three up gap possibilities:

1. If a stock gaps down, and the price continues to fall throughout the day, the candle for the gap day, Day 0, is black. In this case, the price seems to be tumbling down.

2. A stock gaps down and the price moves up during the day, but not enough to fill the initial void on the chart. In this case, the candle on Day 0 is white— perhaps indicating that the downward fall seen at the open has reversed.

3. A stock gaps down with the opening and closing price being identical, resulting in a doji on Day 0.

4. A stock gaps up, but the price moves below the open throughout the day, closing at a price higher than the previous day's high but lower than that day's open. This price action results in an up gap with a black candle on the day of the gap.

5. A stock gaps up with a white candle. When this occurs, the price jumps up at the open and continues to move higher during the day.

6. The stock gaps up with the opening and closing price being identical, resulting in a doji on Day 0.

Table 5.1 summarizes results for each of these six combinations. Eighty-one-and-one-half percent of gap downs are associated with a black candle on the day of the gap. Although these down gaps are more common, they tend to be small in size, 1.24%, relative to the white candle down gaps that average 1.84%. The day of a down gap is a doji only 1.3% of the time; although these are rare, they are the only gaps that have a positive 1-day return. The nominal and market-adjusted returns for buying a stock at the open the day after a downward gapping doji occurs are all positive. Another interesting result about the down gaps is that the 1-day and 3-day nominal returns for the white down gaps are negative, but the 1-day and 3-day market-adjusted returns are positive. This indicates that even though the price of these stocks tended to fall on Day 1, the market, on average, was falling further. All three down gap possibilities had positive nominal and market-adjusted returns by Day 5.

Unlike the gap downs, which are primarily black candle gaps, gap ups tend to occur on white candles. Eighty-three percent of the gap up candles were white. However, at an average size of 1.03%, these gap ups tended to be smaller than the black candle gap ups that averaged 1.51%. It is rare for the candle on the day of a gap up to be a doji; less than 1.4% of the gap ups occur as a doji. The black candle and the white candle gap ups were alike in that they both had negative returns through the 10-day holding period and positive returns for the 30-day holding period. The white candle gap ups, however, did not reverse direction as much on Day 1 and had larger 30-day returns.

Previous Day Candle Color

If you also consider the candle color on Day −1, there are 18 possible cases. Each of the 6 cases just discussed can be preceded by either a white, black, or doji candle day. Table 5.2 reports the results for the 9 possible cases that can occur when the gap is down, and Table 5.3 reports the results for the 9 possible cases than can occur when the gap is up. A designation such as BUW is the notation used for Black-Up-White and means that Day −1 was a black candle, and Day 0 was a gap up white candle day. The other 17 cases are designated in a similar manner.

TABLE 5.1   *Gap Returns Based on Color of Candle on the Day of the Gap*

		Gap Size	Number of Occurrences	Returns					Market-Adjusted Returns				
				1-day	3-day	5-day	10-day	30-day	1-day	3-day	5-day	10-day	30-day
Gap down	All	-1.3394	97029	-0.0204	0.0198	0.3712	0.4793	1.3558	-0.0507	-0.0013	0.0478	0.1116	0.3783
	Black	-1.2372	79061	-0.0240	0.0261	0.3674	0.5019	1.4369	-0.0701	-0.0055	0.0341	0.1200	0.4115
	Doji	-1.1695	1298	0.0555	0.0638	0.3966	0.8705	2.2840	0.1341	0.1660	0.2835	0.5380	1.0722
	White	-1.8370	16670	-0.0088	-0.0136	0.3873	0.3417	0.8986	0.0270	0.0055	0.0942	0.0388	0.1670
Gap up	All	1.1052	11690C3	-0.0903	-0.1802	-0.0229	-0.0474	0.9449	-0.0588	-0.1110	-0.0337	-0.0483	0.3631
	Black	1.5065	17945	-0.2629	-0.2315	-0.1350	-0.2124	0.8213	-0.2190	-0.1819	-0.1586	-0.2821	0.0567
	Doji	1.0910	1621	-0.1651	-0.2151	0.0067	0.3501	1.4648	-0.1153	-0.1828	-0.0702	0.0695	0.1679
	White	1.0315	97337	-0.0573	-0.1702	-0.0028	-0.0236	0.9590	-0.0283	-0.0968	-0.0100	-0.0071	0.4229

TABLE 5.2   *Gap Returns Based on Color of Candle on Day −1 and Day 0 for Down Gaps*

Candle Pattern	Gap Size	Number of Occurences	Returns					Market-Adjusted Returns				
			1-day	3-day	5-day	10-day	30-day	1-day	3-day	5-day	10-day	30-day
All	-1.3394	97,029	-0.0204	0.0198	0.3712	0.4793	1.3558	-0.0507	-0.0013	0.0478	0.1116	0.3783
Black	-1.2372	79,061	-0.0240	0.0261	0.3674	0.5019	1.4369	-0.0701	-0.0055	0.0341	0.1200	0.4115
BDB	-1.1388	64,162	0.0383	0.1271	0.4691	0.6354	1.6878	-0.0225	0.0726	0.1070	0.2081	0.5571
DojiDB	-1.1902	1,195	-0.2617	-0.0648	0.3362	0.6013	2.3031	-0.2525	-0.1665	0.0110	0.1611	0.9611
WDB	-1.7022	13,704	-0.2952	-0.4389	-0.1061	-0.1319	0.1869	-0.2772	-0.3569	-0.3050	-0.2962	-0.3181
White	-1.8370	16,670	-0.0088	-0.0136	0.3873	0.3417	0.8986	0.0270	0.0055	0.0942	0.0388	0.1670
BDW	-1.6548	12,917	0.0340	0.0199	0.4595	0.4073	1.0143	0.0507	0.0173	0.1149	0.0426	0.1238
DojiDW	-2.2576	286	-0.0361	0.1715	0.5265	1.1147	2.8371	-0.0778	0.1478	0.3022	0.7597	1.8701
WDW	-2.4813	3,467	-0.1663	-0.1537	0.1069	0.0336	0.3077	-0.0526	-0.0506	0.0000	-0.0350	0.1875
Doji	-1.1695	1,298	0.0555	0.0638	0.3966	0.8705	2.2840	0.1341	0.1660	0.2835	0.5380	1.0722
BDDoji	-1.1130	1,040	0.1476	0.1319	0.4363	0.7825	1.6947	0.2034	0.1872	0.3121	0.4436	0.3805
DojiDDoji	-0.9003	74	0.0860	0.6192	0.9305	1.8434	6.5473	0.4124	0.9355	1.0294	1.2814	5.1518
WDDoji	-1.5973	184	-0.4774	-0.5443	-0.0421	0.9766	3.9002	-0.3699	-0.2636	-0.1783	0.7722	3.3409

TABLE 5.3 Gap Returns Based on Color of Candle on Day −1 and Day 0 for Up Gaps

Candle Pattern	Gap Size	Number of Occurrences	Returns					Market-Adjusted Returns				
			1-day	3-day	5-day	10-day	30-day	1-day	3-day	5-day	10-day	30-day
All	1.1052	116,903	-0.0903	-0.1802	-0.0229	-0.0474	0.9449	-0.0588	-0.1110	-0.0337	-0.0483	0.3631
Black	1.5065	17,945	-0.2629	-0.2315	-0.1350	-0.2124	0.8213	-0.2190	-0.1819	-0.1586	-0.2821	0.0567
BUB	1.9078	3,680	-0.1521	-0.0358	0.0815	-0.1525	0.5804	-0.1696	-0.0734	-0.0170	-0.1320	-0.0684
DojiUB	1.5070	300	-0.0122	0.4075	0.8101	0.9394	2.0111	0.0468	0.5741	0.8669	0.5869	0.9315
WUB	1.4008	13,965	-0.2975	-0.2968	-0.2123	-0.2529	0.8592	-0.2378	-0.2268	-0.2179	-0.3403	0.0708
White	1.0315	97,337	-0.0573	-0.1702	-0.0028	-0.0236	0.9590	-0.0283	-0.0968	-0.0100	-0.0071	0.4229
BUW	1.3672	17,048	0.0810	0.1316	0.2574	-0.1225	1.0179	0.0858	0.1531	0.1921	0.0288	0.5063
DojiUW	1.0385	1,725	0.0114	0.1976	0.7084	0.5617	1.3793	0.0867	0.2137	0.4694	0.2219	-0.1035
WUW	0.9585	78,564	-0.0888	-0.2437	-0.0748	-0.0150	0.9370	-0.0556	-0.1578	-0.0644	-0.0200	0.4163
Doji	1.0910	1,621	-0.1651	-0.2151	0.0067	0.3501	1.4648	-0.1153	-0.1828	-0.0702	0.0695	0.1679
BUDoji	1.3521	262	-0.0785	-0.1797	0.0828	0.4018	-0.2124	0.0065	-0.1385	-0.0092	0.1422	-1.4909
DojiUDoji	1.2447	96	-0.3149	0.5690	1.2125	2.9354	4.8449	-0.2924	0.5091	1.1236	2.1619	2.3131
WUDoji	1.0251	1,263	-0.1716	-0.2821	-0.1008	0.1429	1.5558	-0.1271	-0.2446	-0.1736	-0.1046	0.3490

When looking at the 18 possible 2-day patterns, which occurs most often? Thirty-seven percent of all gaps follow the White-Up-White pattern. Thus, over one-third of all gaps seen in the market occur on strong upward price movement. The price moves upward on Day –1, jumps up at the open on Day 0, and then continues upward to close higher for Day 0. These gaps average, however, a smaller size than for any of the other 17 combinations except for the extremely rare Doji-Down-Doji pattern.

The second most commonly occurring 2-day pattern is the Black-Down-Black pattern. Twenty-nine percent of the gaps follow this pattern. Like the White-Up-White pattern, the Black-Down-Black pattern also indicates strong price movement, just in a downward direction. The price moves lower during Day–1, the price jumps lower at the open on Day 0, and then the price continues lower during trading on Day 0.

Together, the White-Up-White and Black-Down-White patterns account for two-thirds of the gaps seen in the stock market. What are the rarest patterns to see? Gaps that have a doji on Day –1 or Day 0 rarely occur. Only 3% of the gaps have a doji on either of these days. Of those patterns that do not include a doji, the Black-Up-Black and the White-Down-White patterns are the least common. Less than 2% of gaps follow the Black-Up-Black pattern, but these rare up gaps provide the largest sized up gaps. Slightly rarer, the White-Down-White pattern has the largest gap size, 2.48, of any pattern combination.

Now look more closely at the returns for down gaps presented in Table 5.2. As you saw earlier, down gaps that occur with a black candle average a 1-day return of –0.0240. Looking more closely, however, you can see that this negative return is greatly influenced by those black candle down gaps preceded by a white candle on Day –1. Only 17% of black candle down gaps are preceded by a white candle, but the White-Down-Black pattern has a 1-day return of –0.2952, the lowest of any of the 2-day candle down gap combinations, except the White-Down-Doji pattern. The gap down black candles preceded by a black candle actually have a positive 1-day return of 0.0383. The Black-Down-Black pattern occurs when the price moves lower during the day on Day –1, jumps down at the open on Day 0, and then continues down further during the day to form the second black candle. This pattern sees immediate reversal, with positive 1-day returns. This upward price continues, resulting in the Black-Down-Black having the highest 5-day, 10-day, and 30-day returns of any of the nondoji gap patterns considered. The results for the White-Down-Black pattern are much different; positive returns do not occur until the 30-day holding period; even then, the 30-day return of 0.1869 is the smallest of any of the gap patterns, and the market-adjusted return is still negative.

Interestingly, you can see similar results for the gap down white candle patterns as you did for the gap down black candle patterns. On average, when a stock gaps down on a white candle, the 1-day and 3-day returns are negative. This remains true when the day before the gap is a white candle day, resulting in the White-Down-White pattern having negative 1-day and 3-day returns. This is not the case, however, with the much more frequently occurring Black-Down-White pattern. For the Black-Down-White pattern, the returns and market-adjusted returns for all holding periods considered are positive.

Table 5.3 presents results for up gaps. When all up gaps are lumped together, when black candle up gaps are considered as a group, and when white candle up gaps are grouped together, the 1-day, 3-day, 5-day, and 10-day returns are all negative. Adding the color of the Day −1 candle refines the results a bit. If Day −1 is a white candle day, the results do not change, but if Day −1 is a black candle day, you see a slightly different story. For the Black-Up-White, the 1-day return is 0.0810, the highest for any of the nondoji patterns considered.

Thus, Day −1 color does seem to matter. The general results suggest that shorting a stock the day after it gaps could be a profitable trading strategy. However, if the day before the gap were a black candle, the results in Tables 5.2 and 5.3 suggest considering a long position.

Dramatic Price Move Examples

Now consider some specific examples of dramatic price movements that follow common Black-Down-Black and White-Up-White patterns. By September 15, 2008, American International Group (AIG) was already spinning wildly out of control. In December 2000, AIG peaked at more than 2000. By the beginning of 2002, AIG had fallen below 1500. For about the next 5 years, AIG traded in a range roughly between 1000 and 1500. AIG closed February 2008 below 1000 for the first time since February 2003. By mid-May, AIG had fallen below 800. AIG's steady decline throughout the summer of 2008 is shown in Figure 5.1.

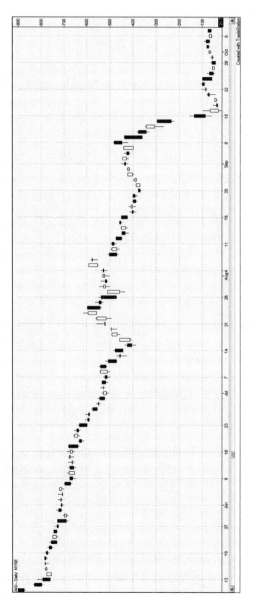

FIGURE 5.1 *Daily stock chart for AIG, May 8–October 7, 2008*

Created with TradeStation

The stock was in free fall. On Friday, September 12, AIG fell from about 300 to close at 234.52. On Monday, September 15, it opened with a gap down of more than 30% and closed down 60.8% from the September 15 close, forming a Black-Down-Black. On September 16, AIG opened at 37, down dramatically from the previous day's close of 95.20. But, September 16 turned out to be a dramatic reversal with the stock closing at 75—more than a 100% increase in one day!

People who say that the stock market is boring just haven't looked closely enough. Take Jammin Java Corporation (JAMN) in May 2011, for instance. If the company's name and ticker symbol make you think of Bob Marley and reggae music, there's a good reason. Jammin Java was founded by Rohan Marley, son of the late Bob Marley and a star linebacker at the University of Miami in the early '90s. On January 10, 2011 JAMN's total volume was a whopping 500 shares and the price was 51 cents. On May 12, the stock gapped up with the price hitting a high of 6.35 per share and closing at 5.42 on volume of more than 20 million shares (see Figure 5.2). The rise was meteoric going from about 1 per share in March to the high of 6.35 in less than 2 months.

But, on May 13, things began to unravel with four consecutive black candle days. The stock fell from an opening price of 5.59 on the 13th to a close of 1.52 on May 18, experiencing an intraday low of 92 cents on the 18th. JAMN's price movement provides an example of what the results in this chapter suggest is a typical price movement after a White-Up-White pattern occurs. Investors who purchased JAMN at the open the day after the gap would experience negative 1-day, 3-day, 5-day, and 10-day returns.

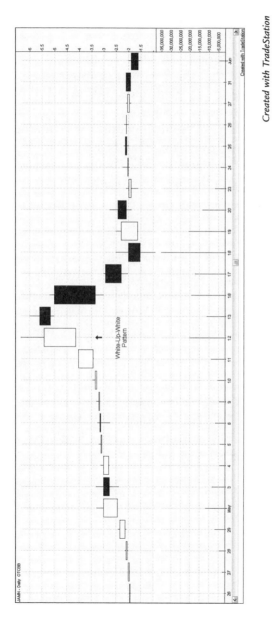

FIGURE 5.2 Daily stock chart for JAMN, May 26–June 1, 2011

On June 14, 2011, JAMN fell below 2; it closed the year at 27 cents per share. What caused this wild ride? The answer isn't clear, but in September there were news reports that the SEC was investigating a possible illegal online pump and dump scheme. The company issued a statement on September 9 saying that they had become aware of some unauthorized Internet stock promotion in May and that Rohan Marley strongly condemned such actions. The company vowed to cooperate fully with the SEC investigation.

JAMN wasn't the only coffee company with a wild ride in 2011. Coffee Holding Company, Inc. (JVA) began the year at 3.85 and ended the year at 7.84, an increase of more than 100%. However, that was nothing compared to what happened in between those dates. On July 11, 2011, the stock hit a high for the year of 30.98, gapping up on a White-Up-White pattern (see Figure 5.3). An investor who saw this pattern might have reasoned that the stock's tripling in price over the prior month was an unsustainable uptrend. Thinking this was an exhaustion gap, the investor might have shorted the stock at the open on July 12 at 29.54 and enjoyed the fall that same day to a close of 22.37. The next 2 days were also black candle days with the stock closing at 18.89 on July 14.

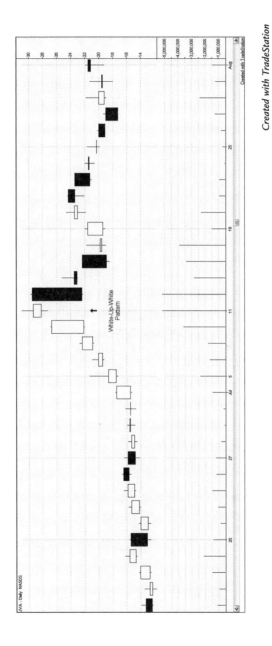

FIGURE 5.3 *Daily stock chart for JVA, May 14–August 1, 2011*

Summary

Gaps have generally been thought of as signaling a strong directional price move. Traditionally, traders have looked for breakaway gaps as a signal that a new trend in the direction of the gap has occurred. In addition, measuring gaps signal that the trend is going to continue in the direction of the gap. Among those who practice Japanese candlestick charting, the adage is "go in the direction of the window."

The results show that price movement does tend to continue downward when a down gap occurs, but only for about a day. You might think that spotting a black candle followed by another black candle that gaps down would be an ominous sign; this might mean that downward price movement is gaining momentum. However, the results show that when a black candle on Day −1 is followed by a gap on Day 0, price movement tends to reverse to an upward direction on Day 1, and this upward movement continues for at least 30 days. This suggests that the downward gap was an overreaction and the price fell too far.

Likewise, you might think that an up gap, especially when it occurs in a White-Up-White pattern, suggests strong upward price momentum. Again, the results bring this traditional reasoning into question. Stocks tend to reverse direction and have negative returns for a couple of weeks following an up gap.

Chapter 6

Gaps and Volume

The previous chapter focused solely on price movement. Price is always the most important variable studied by a technical analyst. After all, it is a change in price that enables a trader to profit. This chapter adds another variable, volume, to the analysis. Volume is simply the number of shares traded over a specific time period, usually a day.

Volume is the oldest confirming indicator used by technical analysts. In 1935, H.M. Gartley provided general rules regarding how to interpret volume.[1] Basically, Gartley suggested that price change on high volume tends to occur in the direction of the trend, and price change on low volume tends to occur on corrective price moves. During an uptrend, higher volume is taken as a sign of active and aggressive interest in owning the stock. However, during a price decline, volume might be light due to a lack of interest in the stock; a lack of potential buyers results in lower trading volume and a falling price.

A number of indexes and oscillators incorporate volume. The most well-known volume-related index is probably On-Balance-Volume (OBV), developed by Joseph Granville in his 1976 book, *A New Strategy of Daily Stock Market Timing for Maximum Profit*.[2] Chaikin Money Flow, the Money Flow Index, and the Elder Force Index are a few examples of volume-related oscillators. Analysts use these indicators to confirm price trends. Volume is a secondary indicator to price analysis; volume cannot be used as a substitute for price analysis.

When using volume statistics, volume-related signals are usually not derived from the volume itself but from a change in the volume. Raw volume numbers measure the liquidity of securities. On a typical day near the end of 2011, the volume for Apple stock was more than 13 million shares. At the same time, the volume for IBM was less than 5 million shares. That Apple had a volume of 13 million shares, more than two-and-one-half times that of IBM, is not meaningful by itself. Knowing that IBM had a volume of 10 million shares on a particular day would be helpful information because it would represent a doubling in volume. If this happened as the price gapped up, you would say that the increased volume confirmed the price movement. The major focus in this chapter addresses the question, "Does volume serve to confirm price movement when stocks gap?"

For example, look at the gap shown in Figure 6.1, which occurred on April 21, 2005, for NYSE Euronext (NYX). Price moved significantly higher on the up gap of almost 40%, but what is so striking is the high volume that occurred that day. More than 14 million shares of NYX traded hands that day. The volume on April 21 was more than 110 times higher than the average volume for the previous 10 days. In the authors' study, NYX had the highest jump in volume relative to the 10-day average volume for any stock.

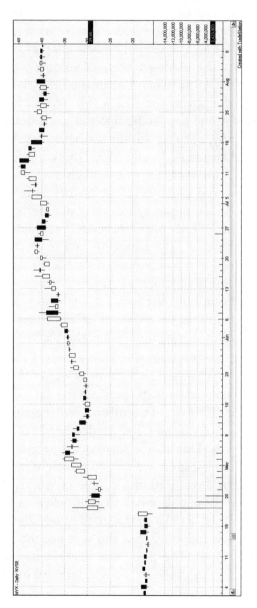

Created with TradeStation

FIGURE 6.1   *Daily stock chart for NYX, April 1–August 9, 2005*

Gaps and a jump in volume are often associated with major news, such as the announcement of a merger, as in the case of NYX. The second highest jump in volume relative to a 10-day moving average of volume occurred on December 17, 1997, when Cincinnati Financial Corp (CINF) gapped up more than 12%. The reason for this gap up was not due to specific financial considerations for the company, such as an announcement of better-than-expected earnings. In late 1995, thinking that the company was not receiving the attention of industry analysts it deserved given its strong history of financial performance, CINF began aggressively marketing itself to Wall Street. CINF was successful at increasing analysts' awareness of the company, and in December, 1997, was added as a component to the S&P500 index. The high-volume December 17 gap is a result of the publicity surrounding the stock's inclusion in the S&P500 index and the purchases of CINF by those who manage portfolios designed to mimic the S&P500.

Figure 6.2 shows that the volume for CINF on December 17 was more than 100 times higher than the volume had averaged over the previous 10 days. To put the volume of CINF for December 17 in perspective, approximately 50% more CINF traded hands that day than IBM shares. Due to the increased interest in the stock, the volume continued to be extremely high for the next several days. Within a couple of weeks, however, the daily volume dropped to well below one million. The increased activity in the stock caused the stock to gap up on December 17, but this was not the beginning of an uptrend. The price was back in its pregap range of $35 by June; in less than 6 months all the price movement of the gap had been lost. This was a case in which a reversal strategy, shorting the stock after the up gap, would have been the profitable tactic.

Extraordinarily high volume can occur on a down gap, also, as shown in Figure 6.3. On January 5, 2007, Herbalife (HLF) gapped down on extremely high volume. The gap was not an unusually large gap (approximately 2%), but the price move that day was significant in that HLF lost about 25% of its value. The volume for the day, more than 22 million shares, was approximately 65 times higher than the average 10-day volume. What caused so much selling of HLF on that day? The company announced that it had lower than expected sales growth during the fourth quarter of 2006 in Mexico, its largest market, and that it expected sales in Mexico to remain flat in 2007. Volume tapered off over the next few trading days, and price remained between 15 and 16 for a month. Because of the positive price movement on January 8, a trader purchasing HLF at the open the day after the gap would have a positive 1-day return of 6.07% and a market-adjusted 1-day return of 5.80%. On February 5, another gap occurred on high volume. This time the gap was up, bringing price up to the level it was at the beginning of January. What caused this second gap? HLF received a buyout offer from Whitney V LP, which owned approximately 27% of the company. Perhaps Whitney wanted to take advantage of the price decline of the previous month, thinking that investors overreacted to the reports in January of lower sales in Mexico. This led to a 19.08% 30-day adjusted market return for investors who purchased HLF at the open on January 8.

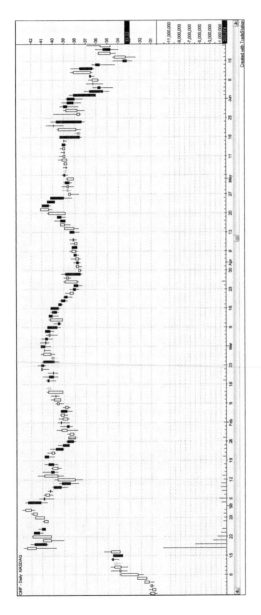

FIGURE 6.2   Daily stock chart for CINF, December 1, 1997–June 19, 1998

Created with TradeStation

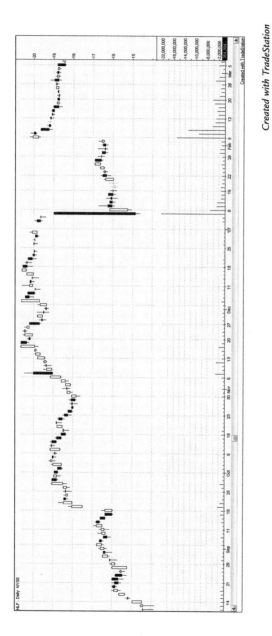

FIGURE 6.3   Daily stock chart for HLF, August 9, 2006–March 5, 2007

You just considered three examples of stocks that had an exceptionally large increase in volume on the day of a gap. This type of increase is often accompanied by a specific, unexpected release of information about the company, such as FDA approval for a new drug, concerns about accounting irregularities, or acquisition possibilities. Sometimes, however, the increase in volume is not so dramatic. News may trickle in over a few days, resulting in increased volume before the entire story is known. For example, rumors of merger talks may result in increased interest in a company over several days with some price movement; then, when the rumors are confirmed, the price jumps further on heavy volume. Or an energy company's stock begins to fall as the result of an oil spill; more selling leads to higher volume. As more news is released, investors realize that the spill is worse than originally thought, causing volume to rise and the price to fall as more investors sell.

You need to consider whether volume is heavier than normal on the day a stock gaps. The question becomes, "How do you measure normal?" You do not want to compare the gap day's volume to the previous day's volume. First, the previous day's volume may also be higher than normal if information is trickling in. Second, the previous day's volume may not be a good measure if there is reason to believe that it is unrepresentatively low. In some instances, investors expect the release of information about a company on a particular day. For example purposes, suppose Merck is scheduled to announce its fourth-quarter earnings on Tuesday. Monday, the market for Merck's stock may be fairly quiet as investors sit on the sidelines waiting for the news. Or the previous day's volume may be unusually low due to shortened holiday hours on the exchange. So, you know that you would want to compare volume on the day of the gap with the "average" volume for the stock. You can do this by comparing a day's volume to a moving average of volume. The shorter the moving average to which you compare the gap day's volume, the more you can look for discrete jumps in volume.

Table 6.1 divides gap downs by volume relative to the 3-, 10-, and 30-day moving averages. As might be expected, more down gaps occur on above average volume than on below average volume. About two-thirds of the gaps occur on above average volume. Furthermore, down gaps that occur on above average volume tend to be larger gaps than down gaps that occur on below average volume. The average size of a down gap is 1.34%; down gaps that occur on relatively low volume average only approximately 0.6%, whereas down gaps occurring on relatively high volume average approximately 1.7%.

You have seen the tendency for down gaps to reverse. Generally, you have seen that a reversal strategy, in this case going long, is more profitable following a down gap than a continuation strategy. The returns in Table 6.1 suggest that this occurs even more quickly for down gaps that occur on low volume. Down gaps that occur on low volume tend to be small gaps, and price tends to rise the following day. The returns for low-volume down gaps are positive at all the return periods considered.

TABLE 6.1   Returns for Down Gaps Occurring at Above Average and Below Average Volume Levels

	Average Gap Size	Number of Occurrences	Returns					Market-Adjusted Returns				
			1-day	3-day	5-day	10-day	30-day	1-day	3-day	5-day	10-day	30-day
All Down Gaps	-1.3394	97,029	-0.0204	0.0198	0.3712	0.4793	1.3558	-0.0507	-0.0013	0.0478	0.1116	0.3783
Volume Lower Than — 3-day Avg	-0.6182	26,632	0.0562	0.1997	0.5514	0.8376	1.7800	-0.0314	0.0489	0.0824	0.1821	0.3196
Volume Lower Than — 10-day Avg	-0.6193	30,823	0.0183	0.2317	0.6220	1.0640	1.7073	-0.0629	0.0278	0.0879	0.2542	0.3000
Volume Lower Than — 30-day Avg	-0.5918	32,307	0.0356	0.1575	0.5521	0.8929	1.8451	-0.0755	-0.0316	0.0163	0.1334	0.2823
Volume Lower Than — 90-day Avg	-0.5719	31,501	0.0056	0.0819	0.4473	0.7408	1.7956	-0.0667	-0.0450	0.0161	0.1245	0.2841
Volume Higher Than — 3-day Avg	-1.6122	70,375	-0.0491	-0.0480	0.3037	0.3454	1.1978	-0.0578	-0.0202	0.0352	0.0867	0.4030
Volume Higher Than — 10-day Avg	-1.6753	66,114	-0.0381	-0.0789	0.2555	0.2068	1.1959	-0.0447	-0.0150	0.0300	0.0449	0.4174
Volume Higher Than — 30-day Avg	-1.7136	64,470	-0.0474	-0.0490	0.2783	0.2686	1.1171	-0.0376	0.0141	0.0610	0.0965	0.4292
Volume Higher Than — 90-day Avg	-1.7101	64,885	-0.0324	-0.0134	0.3246	0.3385	1.1412	-0.0427	0.0171	0.0527	0.0918	0.4218

Down gaps that occur on higher than average volume tend not to reverse until a week out. The 1-day and 3-day returns for the four measures of high-volume gaps are all negative. These down gaps appear to have more initial power behind them; volume is high and the initial price movement on the day of the gap is significant. The momentum behind that gap tends to stay with the stock for a couple of days. However, by Day 5 the story has changed and returns are positive. Interestingly, at the 30-day mark, nominal returns for low-volume down gaps exceed those for high-volume gaps, but the market-adjusted returns for the high-volume gaps are higher.

Now look at how volume impacts the profitability of trading up gaps. Table 6.2 contains information about volume for up gaps. The majority of the 116,903 up gaps occur on relatively high volume. When using the 3-day average volume as the criterion for determining high-volume gaps, 71% of the up gaps are high-volume gaps. Like the down gaps, up gaps that occur on high volume tend to be larger than up gaps that occur on low volume. The average gap size for an up gap is 1.11%; up gaps on low volume tend to be 0.6% or less, whereas up gaps on high volume tend to be more than 1.3%.

As you have seen before, stocks that gap up tend to reverse direction. Investors who go long at the open the day after an up gap have a negative return up to Day 10. Table 6.2 shows this is true for stocks that gap up on both high and low volume. However, the statistics in Figure 6.2 indicate that stocks that gap up on low volume tend to outperform stocks that gap up on high volume by the 30-day time frame. This might seem counterintuitive; you might think that stocks that have a big gap up on high volume have many eager buyers and momentum will push these stocks higher. The counterargument that might explain the results in Table 6.2 is that a large gap on high volume means that all the buyers came in quickly on the same day, and there isn't anything to keep pushing the stock higher. Smaller up gaps on lighter volume may indicate that new information is trickling out to investors and that, as interest in the stock grows, the price will continue to rise.

So far, you have compared sets of stocks that gap on above average volume with those that gap on below average volume. Now break those groups down a bit more, refining your definition of above average and below average volume. In Table 6.3 down gaps are grouped according to the volume on the day of the gap relative to the previous volume for that particular security. Five categories of volume size are considered:

- **Extremely low volume:** Stocks that had a volume on the day of the gap that was less than 25% of the average volume for the security
- **Below average volume:** Stocks that had a volume on the day of the gap that was between 25% and 75% of the average volume for the security
- **Average volume:** Stocks that had a volume on the day of the gap that was within 25% above or below the average volume for the security
- **Above average volume:** Stocks that had a volume on the day of the gap that was between 125% and 175% of the average volume for the security
- **Extremely high volume:** Stocks that had a volume on the day of the gap that was more than 175% of the average volume for the security

TABLE 6.2 *Returns for Up Gaps Occurring at Above Average and Below Average Volume Levels*

| | | Number of Occurrences | Returns | | | | | | Market-Adjusted Returns | | | | | |
	Average Gap Size		1-day	3-day	5-day	10-day	30-day	1-day	3-day	5-day	10-day	30-day
All Up Gaps	1.1052	116,903	-0.0903	-0.1802	-0.0229	-0.0474	0.9449	-0.0588	-0.1110	-0.0337	-0.0483	0.3631
Volume Lower Than												
3-day Avg	0.6094	34,413	-0.1952	-0.3447	-0.2448	-0.1788	1.0468	-0.1097	-0.1666	-0.0953	-0.0665	0.4094
10-day Avg	0.5793	37,117	-0.1119	-0.2701	-0.1033	-0.0521	1.0070	-0.0838	-0.1570	-0.0611	-0.0404	0.2763
30-day Avg	0.5580	39,192	-0.0415	-0.2007	-0.0039	-0.0740	1.0622	-0.0386	-0.1067	0.0025	-0.0312	0.3578
90-day Avg	0.5431	38,830	-0.0329	-0.1100	0.1106	0.0485	1.2486	-0.0248	-0.0571	0.0666	0.0622	0.5203
Volume Higher Than												
3-day Avg	1.3116	82,462	-0.0456	-0.1097	0.0722	0.0098	0.9048	-0.0366	-0.0859	-0.0054	-0.0385	0.3460
10-day Avg	1.3495	79,691	-0.0788	-0.1364	0.0184	-0.0429	0.9214	-0.0458	-0.0875	-0.0172	-0.0499	0.4079
30-day Avg	1.3803	77,394	-0.1149	-0.1679	-0.0254	-0.0291	0.8813	-0.0692	-0.1115	-0.0455	-0.0523	0.3591
90-day Avg	1.3821	77,184	-0.1216	-0.2141	-0.0775	-0.0943	0.7707	-0.0787	-0.1367	-0.0737	-0.1027	0.2582

TABLE 6.3   *Returns for Gap Down Stocks Sorted by Relative Volume*

	Length of Average	Average Gap Size	Number of Occurrences	Returns					Market-Adjusted Returns				
				1-day	3-day	5-day	10-day	30-day	1-day	3-day	5-day	10-day	30-day
Extremely Low Volume	3-day	-0.8973	100	-0.3768	-0.5998	0.0007	-0.5966	-2.4567	-0.0174	-0.4442	-0.3034	-1.3667	-3.9657
	10-day	-0.5529	94	-0.3773	0.1790	2.0027	1.5557	2.5344	-0.0317	0.0253	1.7732	0.7232	0.8090
	30-day	-0.4840	77	-0.6434	0.1844	0.5955	0.4680	2.4559	-0.5579	-0.1781	0.0695	-0.4194	0.6680
	90-day	-0.6167	73	-0.4793	0.7860	1.0030	-0.3604	1.6327	-0.5380	0.4070	0.3969	-0.8391	0.0675
Below Average Volume	3-day	-0.6035	10,435	0.0581	0.2973	0.5747	0.8786	1.8520	-0.0200	0.1024	0.1434	0.2220	0.3268
	10-day	-0.6066	12,592	-0.0061	0.3073	0.6740	1.2349	1.6026	-0.0945	0.0582	0.1489	0.3519	0.2115
	30-day	-0.5672	14,298	0.0664	0.2455	0.5784	1.0544	2.0037	-0.1011	-0.0260	0.0255	0.1827	0.3027
	90-day	-0.5373	14,311	0.0080	0.0511	0.4041	0.8160	2.0560	-0.0819	-0.1072	-0.0434	0.0820	0.3138
Average Volume	3-day	-0.6573	53,315	0.0375	0.0968	0.5387	0.7369	1.6672	-0.0391	0.0344	0.0808	0.1607	0.3207
	10-day	-0.6564	34,948	0.0458	0.1666	0.5810	0.8102	1.7395	-0.0327	0.0284	0.0729	0.1708	0.3980
	30-day	-0.6548	33,934	-0.0050	0.1103	0.5341	0.7193	1.6252	-0.0495	0.0163	0.0527	0.1481	0.3555
	90-day	-0.6443	32,534	-0.0101	0.0879	0.4451	0.5813	1.4657	-0.0605	0.0082	0.0320	0.1008	0.2819
Above Average Volume	3-day	-0.8225	23,161	0.0272	0.0720	0.5569	0.6035	1.5438	-0.0063	0.0685	0.1504	0.2276	0.6209
	10-day	-0.8345	20,436	-0.0035	-0.0262	0.4564	0.4188	1.4890	-0.0220	0.0523	0.1319	0.1801	0.5009
	30-day	-0.8526	19,571	-0.0299	-0.0139	0.4347	0.4803	1.3278	-0.0061	0.0797	0.1481	0.2064	0.5327
	90-day	-0.8319	19,330	-0.0249	0.0266	0.4764	0.5591	1.2774	-0.0358	0.0539	0.1047	0.1795	0.4738
Extremely High Volume	3-day	-2.7533	29,996	-0.1470	-0.1999	-0.0262	-0.0341	0.7218	-0.1082	-0.1293	-0.0990	-0.0619	0.2932
	10-day	-2.8464	28,867	-0.1168	-0.2509	-0.0777	-0.2113	0.6945	-0.0732	-0.1015	-0.0898	-0.1160	0.3450
	30-day	-2.8564	28,897	-0.0710	-0.1753	0.0288	-0.0955	0.7494	-0.0546	-0.0636	-0.0206	-0.0385	0.3433
	90-day	-2.7936	30,138	-0.0397	-0.0813	0.1849	0.1304	0.9519	-0.0332	-0.0038	0.0482	0.0669	0.4476

For each of the five categories, we measure the average volume in four different ways: 3-day, 10-day, 30-day, and 90-day average volume. About one-third of the down gaps occur on average volume. At least 29% of down gaps occur on what we categorize as extremely high volume. Very few of the down gaps, less than 0.1%, occur on extremely low volume. Consistent with previous results you have seen, Figure 6.3 indicates that the higher the relative volume on the day of the gap, the bigger the gap; the gap size for average volume gaps tends to be approximately 0.66%, whereas the gap size for the above average volume group is in the 0.82%–0.85% range. The gap size for extremely high volume down gaps is in the 2.7%–2.9% range.

As you have seen several times, stocks that gap down on Day 0 tend to move lower during the day on Day 1. This relationship generally holds true for stocks that gap down on high volume and on low volume; especially when market adjusted returns are considered. Stocks that gap down on volume that is 75% below the average 3-day volume or lower behave differently than most gap down stocks in that returns remain negative over longer holding periods. The 30-day market-adjusted return for this group is –3.9657%. This would suggest a profitable shorting strategy for stocks that gap down on extremely low volume; however, with a sample size of 100, there are not enough observations upon which to build a trading strategy. The market-adjusted returns all the average volume and above average volume down gap categories were positive at the 3-day, 5-day, 10-day, and 30-day points.

Table 6.4 provides a similar analysis for stocks that gap up. About 35% of the up gaps occur on average volume. Again you can see that gaps that occur on higher volume tend to be larger gaps. The up gaps occurring on average volume tend to be approximately 0.64%, whereas the up gaps that occur at extremely high-volume levels average at least 2.08%.

Table 6.4 contains a high number of negative returns. When you consider all the up gaps lumped together, you find that 1-, 3-, 5-, and 10-day nominal returns and market-adjusted returns were negative. This pattern appears to hold true regardless of volume on the day of the gap. The additional information that Table 6.4 provides is that if a stock gaps up on extremely low volume, price reverses and continues downward over the next 30 days. Stocks that gap up on average volume do not see positive market-adjusted returns until after 10 days, but these are the strongest performers at the 30-day mark.

Summary

This chapter considered a classic variable used by technical analysts to confirm price movements: volume. Traditional analysis suggests that price movements, especially upward movements, on high volume are more meaningful than when they occur on low volume. However, the analysis in this chapter suggests that volume does not provide a great deal of useful information or added value. We determined in earlier chapters that gap downs tend to be followed by continued price declines on Day 1, but prices quickly reversed. The biggest insight that volume gives you is that price reversal tends to occur sooner for down gaps that occur on moderately low volume than for those occurring on high volume. Table 6.1, shows that low-volume down gaps tend to reverse on Day 1, whereas high-volume down gaps tend not to reverse until after Day 3.

TABLE 6.4 Returns for Gap Up Stocks Sorted by Relative Volume

	Length of Average	Average Gap Size	Number of Occurrences	Returns					Market Adjusted Returns				
				1-day	3-day	5-day	10-day	30-day	1-day	3-day	5-day	10-day	30-day
Extremely Low Volume	3-day	0.9424	118	-1.0252	-2.1313	-1.7085	-3.4945	-3.7402	-0.1261	-0.5541	-0.7063	-0.4993	-1.1495
	10-day	0.5164	93	-1.1608	-2.6022	-2.0957	-4.1074	-5.2670	-0.7031	-1.6121	-1.6488	-2.1953	-3.1623
	30-day	0.5266	88	-0.9484	-1.1462	-0.9807	-1.6770	-1.5166	-0.5744	-0.4768	-0.0099	-0.1548	-0.2630
	90-day	0.5178	84	-0.4658	-0.8396	-0.6520	-2.6832	-8.1408	-0.1773	-0.2487	-0.3278	-1.0666	-5.8882
Below Average Volume	3-day	0.6001	13,586	-0.2911	-0.4678	-0.4588	-0.4199	0.7696	-0.1844	-0.2308	-0.1782	-0.1447	0.2036
	10-day	0.5314	14,900	-0.1670	-0.3901	-0.3202	-0.2564	0.6873	-0.1293	-0.2048	-0.1341	-0.1219	0.1082
	30-day	0.5103	16,949	-0.0505	-0.2708	-0.1395	-0.2647	0.7570	-0.0456	-0.1138	-0.0180	-0.0316	0.2503
	90-day	0.4913	16,991	-0.0475	-0.0878	0.0938	0.0004	1.2287	-0.0334	0.0282	0.0913	0.0996	0.5401
Average Volume	3-day	0.6491	41,668	-0.1037	-0.2250	-0.0094	0.0226	1.1529	-0.0602	-0.1298	-0.0263	-0.0226	0.4695
	10-day	0.6526	43,448	-0.0697	-0.1831	0.0452	0.0648	1.2601	-0.0435	-0.1263	-0.0226	-0.0074	0.4833
	30-day	0.6379	42,851	-0.0427	-0.1374	0.0971	0.0666	1.2707	-0.0266	-0.0890	0.0192	-0.0020	0.4762
	90-day	0.6331	41,417	-0.0338	-0.1603	0.0380	-0.0168	1.1181	-0.0204	-0.1007	-0.0152	-0.0498	0.3982
Above Average Volume	3-day	0.8434	27,683	-0.0577	-0.1686	0.0167	-0.0723	0.8754	-0.0567	-0.1525	-0.1012	-0.1379	0.3073
	10-day	0.8593	25,518	-0.0714	-0.1423	0.0260	-0.1791	0.7869	-0.0356	-0.0919	-0.0489	-0.1852	0.2219
	30-day	0.8791	24,399	-0.1283	-0.1979	-0.0701	-0.1232	0.6804	-0.0773	-0.1445	-0.1175	-0.1695	0.1300
	90-day	0.8631	23,954	-0.1026	-0.2176	-0.0544	-0.0516	0.7391	-0.0567	-0.1159	-0.0495	-0.0715	0.2230
Extremely High Volume	3-day	2.0837	33,820	-0.0143	-0.0078	0.1152	0.0542	0.8382	-0.0057	0.0004	0.0792	0.0391	0.3524
	10-day	2.1553	32,849	-0.0908	-0.0990	-0.0010	0.0184	0.7985	-0.0599	-0.0638	0.0224	0.0486	0.4500
	30-day	2.2050	32,299	-0.1430	-0.1687	-0.0666	-0.0112	0.8077	-0.0935	-0.1084	-0.0333	0.0110	0.4341
	90-day	2.1591	33,568	-0.1777	-0.2198	-0.1043	-0.0967	0.7080	-0.1266	-0.1586	-0.0837	-0.0995	0.2863

Endnotes

1. Gartley, H.M. *Profits in the Stock Market*, 3rd ed. (1981). Pomeroy, WA: Lambert-Gann Publishing Co., 1935.

2. Granville, Joseph. *A New Strategy of Daily Stock Market Timing for Maximum Profit*. Englewood Cliffs, NJ: Prentice-Hall, Inc., 1976.

Chapter 7

Gaps and Moving Averages

Chapter 5, "Gaps and Previous Price Movement," examined the relationship between gaps and price movements immediately around the time of the gap. Specifically, you looked at candle colors on the day before the gap and the day of the gap. You saw that noting the color of the candle the day before a gap occurred did help determine profitable trading strategies. When you saw a black candle on Day –1 and a gap on Day 0, the returns on Day 1 tended to be positive. This was especially true for down gaps, suggesting that when downward price movement on Day -1 is followed by a down gap on Day 0, much of the downward pressure on price is exhausted and a reversal is likely.

This chapter takes a slightly longer-term view. What if the stock's price is above (or below) its 10-day moving average on the day of the gap? How is that related to price movements after the day of the gap? Similarly, what is the impact of the stock's 10-day, 30-day, or 90-day moving average price? Basically, this chapter considers how gaps that occur at relatively high prices compare to gaps that occur at relatively low prices.

Calculation of a Moving Average

Technical analysts have used moving averages for many decades to smooth erratic data and to make it easier to view underlying trends. A moving average is simply an average over some past window of time calculated in successive time periods. For example, suppose the closing prices for a stock each day over a week are the following:

Monday	25
Tuesday	26
Wednesday	27
Thursday	28
Friday	29

On Wednesday, the 3-day average price would be 26. After the close on Thursday, the 3-day average would be calculated using Tuesday's, Wednesday's, and Thursday's closing prices; thus it would be 27. The 3-day average on Friday would be the average of 27, 28, and 29, which is 28. Therefore, the 3-day moving average closing prices for Wednesday, Thursday, and Friday would be 26, 27, and 28, respectively. This type of moving average, in which each time period is equally weighted, is referred to as a **simple moving average**. At times, technical analysts use more sophisticated moving averages, such as a linearly weighted moving average or an exponentially smoothed moving average. For more detailed information on the calculation of various types of moving averages, see the discussion provided by Charles Kirkpatrick and Julie Dahlquist in their book, *Technical Analysis: The Complete Resource for Financial Market Technicians.*[1]

To do this, we calculate 10-day, 30-day, and 90-day simple moving averages. For the 10-day moving average, we computed a simple moving average of the closing prices from Day −10 through Day −1. We then examined the relationship between the price on the day of the gap and the moving average of price in several ways. To explain, say that the 10-day moving average as of Day −1 was 13 and that the closing price on Day 0 (the day of the gap) was 10. In this instance, the Day 0 price would be below the 10-day moving average of 13, and the gap would be classified as occurring below the moving average.[2]

Table 7.1 shows the average returns for holding periods of 1, 3, 5, 10, and 30 days following the day of a down gap when the gap occurs below and above price moving average. When all 97,029 down gaps are considered, the 1-day return the day of the gap is negative. As you have seen before, when a down gap occurs, the price usually continues downward on Day 1 but quickly reverses and begins rising. What is striking about the results in Table 7.1 is this holds true for down gaps that occur below the price moving average but not for down gaps that occur above the price moving average.

Now look a little more closely at the down gaps that occur at prices below the moving averages. Eighty-eight percent of down gaps occur at a price below the 10-day moving average; 73% and 61% fall below the 30-day and the 90-day moving average, respectively. Thus, most down gaps occur at a below average price. Also, notice that the down gaps that occur at below average prices tend to be larger than the down gaps that occur at above average prices. For the down gaps occurring at below average prices, the 3-day return is also negative.

TABLE 7.1   *Returns for Down Gaps Occurring Below and Above Price Moving Average*

		Gap Size	Number of Occurrences	Returns					Market-Adjusted Returns				
				1-day	3-day	5-day	10-day	30-day	1-day	3-day	5-day	10-day	30-day
All Down Gaps		-1.3394	97,029	-0.0204	0.0198	0.3712	0.4793	1.3558	-0.0507	-0.0013	0.0478	0.1116	0.3783
Below Moving Average	10-day SMA	-1.4360	85,505	-0.0285	-0.0077	0.3712	0.4491	1.4573	-0.0597	-0.0091	0.0442	0.1061	0.4161
	30-day SMA	-1.5598	70,474	-0.0693	-0.1351	0.2325	0.3417	1.3093	-0.0983	-0.0865	-0.0642	-0.0051	0.3019
	90-day SMA	-1.6669	59,279	-0.0548	-0.0761	0.2945	0.2707	1.0753	-0.1084	-0.0659	-0.0649	-0.0568	0.1672
Above Moving Average	10-day SMA	-0.6185	11,432	0.0426	0.2260	0.3783	0.7059	0.6195	0.0180	0.0560	0.0796	0.1509	0.1108
	30-day SMA	-0.7478	26,303	0.1132	0.4354	0.7373	0.8393	1.4963	0.0783	0.2274	0.3416	0.4141	0.5899
	90-day SMA	-0.8127	37,107	0.0356	0.1677	0.4768	0.7883	1.8019	0.0418	0.0969	0.2095	0.3570	0.7116

Fewer stocks tend to gap down at an above average price. Only 12%, 27%, and 38% of the stocks gapped down at a price above the 10-day, 30-day, and 90-day moving average, respectively. The stocks that gap down at an above average price, tend to have small gaps. Most surprisingly, Table 7.1 shows that stocks that gap down at an above average price have, on average, a positive price movement on Day 1. All three of the down gaps at above average price subgroups have positive returns for 1-day through the 30-day holding periods. These results suggest that purchasing stocks that down gap at prices above a 10-day, 30-day, or 90-day moving average would be a profitable strategy.

Now turn your attention to stocks that gap up at above average and at below average prices. Table 7.2 shows the results for these stocks. Up gaps occur 116,903 times in the sample; the average gap size is 1.11%. Returns for stocks that gap up are negative up to the 10-day holding period; thus stocks tend to reverse right after gapping up. Unlike down gaps, most up gaps occur at an above average price. In fact, 89% of up gaps occur at a price higher than the 10-day moving average. Up gaps also tend to be slightly larger if they occur at an above average price. Although all subsets of upward gapping stocks in the test have negative 1-day and 3-day returns, the absolute values of the returns for the stocks gapping up above the moving average is significantly lower than those gapping below their moving average price. This suggests more profitable results from shorting stocks that gap up below their moving average than those that gap up above their moving average. Also, the reversal from negative returns to positive returns comes much sooner for the stocks that gap up at above average prices. For example, stocks that gap up at a price above their 30-day or 90-day moving average have positive returns by the 5-day holding period.

Merely looking to see if the price is above or below its moving average, as you have just done, ignores the amount by which that price is greater or less than its average. Tables 7.1 and 7.2 lump stocks that gap at a price one cent above their price moving average with those that gap at a price that is twice their price moving average. To refine this categorization a bit more, we break the groups into five categories. If a gap occurs within 75% to 125% of its moving average, it is placed in the gap at an "average price" category. If a gap occurs at a price level that is 125% to 175% of the moving average, it is categorized as an "above average price" gap. Gaps that occur at a price level that is more than 175% of the moving average are classified as "extremely high price" gaps. Likewise, stocks that gap at a price that is between 25% and 75% of the moving average are classified as "below average price" gaps; gaps occurring at a price less than 25% of the moving average are referred to as "extremely low price" gaps.

Table 7.3 contains the results for these five categories for down gaps. As you can see, most gaps occur within 75% to 125% of the moving average for the stock. Gap downs at above average and below average prices tend to be larger gaps, with the largest gap sizes occurring at the extreme prices. Looking at the average price gaps, you can see that a down gap on Day 0 is likely to be followed by downward price movement on Day 1; however, these stocks quickly reverse, leading to positive 10- and 30-day market-adjusted returns for these stocks.

TABLE 7.2 Returns for Up Gaps Occurring Below and Above Price Moving Average

		Gap Size	Number of Occurrences	Returns					Market-Adjusted Returns				
				1-day	3-day	5-day	10-day	30-day	1-day	3-day	5-day	10-day	30-day
All Up Gaps		1.1052	116,903	-0.0903	-0.1802	-0.0229	-0.0474	0.9449	-0.0588	-0.1110	-0.0337	-0.0483	0.3631
Below Moving Average	10-day SMA	0.7913	13,204	-0.3460	-0.2253	-0.0619	-0.2377	1.8713	-0.2074	-0.1416	-0.0828	-0.1500	0.6381
	30-day SMA	0.9418	27,532	-0.2662	-0.3018	-0.2391	-0.4847	1.1360	-0.1659	-0.2326	-0.2247	-0.4474	0.1895
	90-day SMA	1.0760	35,810	-0.1933	-0.3503	-0.1989	-0.3162	0.7045	-0.0988	-0.1770	-0.1054	-0.2205	0.1734
Above Moving Average	10-day SMA	1.1447	103,604	-0.0566	-0.1729	-0.0150	-0.0214	0.8310	-0.0388	-0.1055	-0.0246	-0.0337	0.3314
	30-day SMA	1.1540	89,054	-0.0358	-0.1409	0.0502	0.0920	0.8822	-0.0258	-0.0720	0.0310	0.0791	0.4110
	90-day SMA	1.1126	80,204	-0.0467	-0.1029	0.0677	0.0739	1.0317	-0.0436	-0.0802	0.0084	0.0297	0.4230

TABLE 7.3   Returns for Gap Downs Sorted by Relative Price Level

		Average Gap Size	Number of Occurences	Returns					Market-Adjusted Returns				
				1-day	3-day	5-day	10-day	30-day	1-day	3-day	5-day	10-day	30-day
Extremely Low Price	MA10	-50.4984	17	9.7400	-3.4483	4.5993	15.7905	-3.6105	9.3072	-3.7299	5.1828	18.3486	5.5856
	MA30	-40.7324	26	4.8749	-2.0648	6.7527	14.2786	4.3419	4.4487	-2.6637	6.2854	15.4389	11.1936
	MA90	-15.8923	126	0.0418	3.2977	10.8941	9.9442	27.9122	-0.4593	1.8891	8.3283	8.5821	26.6791
Below Average Price	MA10	-9.9963	2,385	0.1971	1.1745	2.6800	1.5129	3.0809	0.0906	1.3183	2.0424	1.3723	3.1771
	MA30	-6.0698	4,866	-0.1522	-0.2584	1.6772	1.3780	1.5889	-0.2370	0.3010	1.1518	1.1340	1.9511
	MA90	-3.8516	9,477	-0.2001	-0.4200	0.6672	0.3854	0.9504	-0.3379	-0.1434	0.1353	0.1822	0.8863
Average Price	MA10	-1.1115	94,496	-0.0281	-0.0091	0.3123	0.4510	1.3211	-0.0566	-0.0344	-0.0036	0.0770	0.3137
	MA30	-1.0742	91,482	-0.0179	0.0290	0.2884	0.4078	1.3316	-0.0460	-0.0211	-0.0232	0.0358	0.2798
	MA90	-1.0341	83,995	-0.0130	0.0380	0.2907	0.4278	1.2965	-0.0332	-0.0089	-0.0046	0.0528	0.2287
Above Average Price	MA10	-3.1417	34	0.5707	0.7502	0.3028	-0.9502	-11.7538	0.7078	0.4487	-0.2412	-2.2527	-13.1494
	MA30	-1.6805	377	0.6592	1.3535	2.8151	4.9753	5.8050	0.7465	0.9242	2.1398	3.8905	4.3977
	MA90	-1.2185	2,571	0.3544	0.7147	1.1365	1.6919	3.9630	0.3786	0.5528	0.7839	1.1051	2.5948
Extremely High Price	MA10	-3.0443	5	9.3487	3.3321	14.4500	1.3369	-8.5585	9.8077	4.1425	15.4778	3.0748	-4.8833
	MA30	-3.8162	26	3.6476	2.8120	-0.0400	-3.9341	-8.5660	3.9497	2.7774	0.2258	-4.9684	-9.8050
	MA90	-2.1834	217	0.6867	1.1398	0.5284	0.5079	-4.6137	0.9489	0.6324	-0.1544	-0.9399	-6.0966

Remember that in Table 7.1 you saw that down gaps that occurred above moving averages had positive returns out to the 30-day holding period. Tweaking the definition of "above average" a bit in Table 7.3 provides some useful information. The 1-day and the 3-day returns for stocks in the above average price and the extremely high price categories are positive, consistent with the results from Table 7.1. However, Table 7.3 warns that while these positive returns continue on average for stocks that gap down at a high price, positive returns do not continue to the 30-day holding period for all the subgroups. Stocks that gap down at extremely high prices tend to have large, negative returns by the 30-day holding period. The data in Table 7.3 suggests that traders should carefully watch stocks that have large gap downs at relatively high prices.

Table 7.4 presents the results for up gaps broken down into the five categories. The vast majority of up gaps occur within 75% to 125% of the moving average. Gaps that occur further away from the moving average, whether above or below, tend to be larger gaps. Looking at Table 7.4, it is striking how many negative return numbers are in the table. These results suggest that taking a long position immediately after a gap up in the price is not prudent, regardless of the price level at which the gap occurs. The one exception to this is the group of stocks that gapped up at a price less than 25% of their 30-day moving average; these stocks had astonishingly high returns. But, before you get too excited about these results, consider that there were only three occurrences of stocks gapping up at a price that was less than 25% of its 30-day moving average between 1995 and 2011. Not only is this situation rare, but also a sample size of three is not large enough from which to draw conclusions upon which to base trades.

TABLE 7.4   *Returns for Gap Ups Sorted by Relative Price Level*

		Average Gap Size	Number of Occurences	Returns					Market-Adjusted Returns				
				1-day	3-day	5-day	10-day	30-day	1-day	3-day	5-day	10-day	30-day
Extremely Low Price	MA10		-										
	MA30	11.1950	3	16.4152	128.3480	101.1841	62.7990	25.8791	17.4927	131.5065	105.1838	69.8725	39.7867
	MA90	5.9088	32	-0.5241	14.8102	13.7560	9.3724	14.5756	-0.8266	15.5931	14.8028	12.0809	17.8028
Below Average Price	MA10	3.9982	50	-0.7358	5.4899	3.5050	-0.8748	-2.9910	-0.4045	6.1948	4.0808	0.1407	-2.1029
	MA30	2.6355	603	-1.9354	-2.7376	-2.6465	-4.2718	0.1055	-1.2210	-1.7116	-1.6403	-1.9955	1.5038
	MA90	1.9666	3,321	-0.5965	-0.7375	-0.4949	-0.8585	2.6813	-0.1942	-0.2247	0.2042	0.0444	3.0454
Average Price	MA10	1.0009	113,981	-0.0602	-0.1367	0.0251	-0.0177	0.9488	-0.0314	-0.0725	0.0043	-0.0222	0.3585
	MA30	0.9787	110,239	-0.0536	-0.1199	0.0181	-0.0305	0.9294	-0.0251	-0.0618	-0.0012	-0.0389	0.3341
	MA90	0.9407	99,063	-0.0316	-0.1080	0.0424	0.0189	0.8636	-0.0115	-0.0547	-0.0018	-0.0189	0.2259
Above Average Price	MA10	4.9208	2,635	-0.9569	-1.4664	-1.3631	-0.5171	1.4200	-0.8271	-1.1858	-0.9588	-0.3725	1.1379
	MA30	3.1036	5,306	-0.3295	-0.7072	-0.0296	0.5505	1.7280	-0.3317	-0.5323	-0.0217	0.4624	1.1370
	MA90	1.8770	12,185	-0.2432	-0.3986	-0.1617	-0.1805	1.2867	-0.2314	-0.3332	-0.1436	-0.1425	0.8650
Extremely High Price	MA10	12.6614	142	-7.1137	-12.1675	-12.7449	-13.5967	-6.5414	-6.8899	-12.1702	-12.7199	-13.8457	-6.9864
	MA30	6.2398	435	-4.0070	-6.0264	-6.1091	-5.3296	-4.4447	-3.8114	-5.8315	-5.7638	-5.6101	-4.7542
	MA90	3.5248	1,413	-1.8201	-2.3063	-1.9206	-1.7865	-1.8622	-1.7028	-2.1582	-1.6502	-1.7240	-2.4599

To understand a bit more about how a gap in the stock price can be related to moving averages, look at Figure 7.1. This chart is a daily candlestick chart for Netlist Inc. (NLST) over approximately 3 months. NLST designs, manufactures, and sells memory subsystems for datacenter server, high-performance computing, and communications markets. In mid-November 2009, the stock suddenly became more heavily traded. The daily volume, which had averaged below 400,000, jumped to more than 10 million on Friday, November 13, and to more than 25 million on Monday, November 16. This heavy volume can be attributed to new interest in the stock as the company announced the introduction of a new computer memory module. Not only did volume rise significantly, but price rose significantly. NLST had been trading under $1 a share for months but reached almost $5 a share on Friday, November 13. Figure 7.1 shows three moving averages, a 10-day, a 30-day, and a 90-day simple moving average. The rapidly rising price of NLST started pulling the moving averages up. The 10-day moving average (MA) moved up the most, closely tracking the price movement. The rise in the 30-day MA is much more subtle.

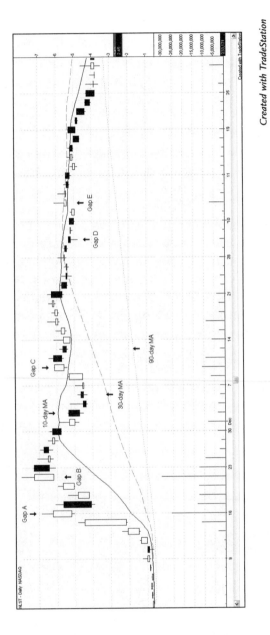

FIGURE 7.1   Daily stock chart for NLST, November 2, 2009–January 28, 2010

On Monday, December 16, NLST gapped up. This gap, labeled Gap A in Figure 7.1, occurred above all three moving averages. This gap falls into the gap at an "extremely high price" category. Of the entire sample, this gap tops the list as the highest percentage above the 30-day moving average. It is the second highest above the 10-day moving average and the third highest above the 90-day moving average. As you have seen often happens, the price moves down the following day. After two white candles on Days 2 and 3, NLST gaps up again on Day 4, Friday, December 20. This is another gap at an extremely high price relative to the moving averages; it ranks fifth on the list of gaps relative to the 30-day moving average and on the 90-day moving average list. The following trading day, you can see another black candle. At this point NLST's uptrend has lost its steam. By November 30, the 10-day MA has flattened out and the price falls below the moving average. On December 9, the stock gaps up again. This gap, labeled Gap C in Figure 7.1 crosses above the 10-day MA. Gap C is clearly above the 30-day and 90-day moving averages. The candle on December 9 crossed above the 10-day moving average, and NLST closed above the moving average; thus, you can classify this gap as occurring above the 10-day MA. NLST trades at approximately 6 for the next couple of weeks. Then, on December 30, Gap D occurs. This down gap is an example of a situation in which a gap is classified differently depending on which moving average is used. Gap D occurs at a below average price when the 10-day or the 30-day moving average is considered; it occurs at an above average price when the slower 90-day moving average is the criterion. Four days later another gap, labeled Gap E, occurs. This gap up occurs above the

30-day and 90-day moving averages but below the faster 10-day moving average.

So far, the analysis of trading strategies has considered the location of a gap relative to one moving average. If considering one moving average adds value to the decision, would considering two or three be even better? In other words, what if the price is not just below the 10-day moving average but is also below its 30-day moving average? Remember the gaps in NLST you just considered in Figure 7.1. Three of the gaps pictured, Gaps A, B, and C, are classified as above the 10-day, above the 30-day, and above the 90-day moving average. Gap D is included in the above 90-day moving average grouping but in the below 10-day moving average and 30-day moving average categories. Gap E is above the 10-day and 90-day moving average but below the 30-day moving average.

Looking at combinations of moving averages does seem to make a difference. Consider the results presented in Table 7.5. Of the 97,029 down gaps, 85,505 occur below the 10-day moving average and 70,474 occur below the 30-day moving average. However, only 68,203 down gaps occur below both the 10-day and the 30-day moving averages. Thus, you must consider that the gaps occurring below the 30-day moving average are not simply a subset of those occurring below the 10-day moving average; clearly, some down gaps occur below the 30-day moving average but above the 10-day moving average. Gap E in Figure 7.1 is an example of such a gap. Almost one-fourth of the down gaps that lie below the 10-day and 30-day moving averages occur above the 90-day moving average.

TABLE 7.5   Returns for Down Gaps Occurring Below and Above Multiple Price Moving Averages

		Gap Size	Number of Occurrences	Returns					Market-Adjusted Returns				
				1-day	3-day	5-day	10-day	30-day	1-day	3-day	5-day	10-day	30-day
All Down Gaps		-1.3394	97,029	-0.0204	0.0198	0.3712	0.4793	1.3558	-0.0507	-0.0013	0.0478	0.1116	0.3783
Below Moving Average	10-day SMA	-1.4360	85,505	-0.0285	-0.0077	0.3712	0.4491	1.4573	-0.0597	-0.0091	0.0442	0.1061	0.4161
	30-day SMA	-1.5598	70,474	-0.0693	-0.1351	0.2325	0.3417	1.3093	-0.0983	-0.0865	-0.0642	-0.0051	0.3019
	90-day SMA	-1.6669	59,279	-0.0548	-0.0761	0.2945	0.2707	1.0753	-0.1084	-0.0659	-0.0649	-0.0568	0.1672
	10/30 combo	-1.5894	68,203	-0.0728	-0.1411	0.2368	0.3219	1.3363	-0.0980	-0.0761	-0.0509	0.0057	0.3171
	10/90 combo	-1.7295	55,714	-0.0632	-0.0970	0.2908	0.2446	1.1578	-0.1129	-0.0637	-0.0618	-0.0549	0.2178
	10/30/90 combo	-1.7803	52,237	-0.0816	-0.1607	0.2327	0.2210	1.1325	-0.1251	-0.0924	-0.0912	-0.0726	0.1945
Above Moving Average	10-day SMA	-0.6185	11,432	0.0426	0.2260	0.3783	0.7059	0.6195	0.0180	0.0560	0.0796	0.1509	0.1108
	30-day SMA	-0.7478	26,303	0.1132	0.4354	0.7373	0.8393	1.4963	0.0783	0.2274	0.3416	0.4141	0.5899
	90-day SMA	-0.8127	37,107	0.0356	0.1677	0.4768	0.7883	1.8019	0.0418	0.0969	0.2095	0.3570	0.7116
	10/30 combo	-0.6023	9,134	0.0449	0.2675	0.4362	0.6556	0.6452	0.0485	0.1637	0.2025	0.2731	0.1669
	10/90 combo	-0.5799	7,778	0.0270	0.2157	0.3695	0.6914	0.9405	0.0419	0.1253	0.1454	0.2318	0.3876
	10/30/90 combo	-0.5827	7,248	0.0364	0.2724	0.4355	0.7324	0.9620	0.0464	0.1728	0.2105	0.3050	0.4190

The most stringent requirements for categorizing a gap as occurring at a below average price is the requirement that the gap lie below the 10-day, 30-day, and 90-day moving averages. Over half of all down gaps fall into this category. One interesting result presented in Table 7.5 is that the gaps that meet this stringent requirement have the largest negative 1-day return; actually, the negative return is four times larger than the negative return for the entire set of down gaps. These results reinforce the idea that down gaps that occur at below average prices should be sold short at the open of the next trading day for a short-run return.

Remember that gap downs that occur at above average prices tend to experience price reversal the next day, suggesting a long position strategy. A minority of stocks that gap down do so at above average prices. The results in Table 7.5 indicate that adding more stringent requirements, such as that the gap must occur above all three moving averages, does not add any value. Those down gaps occurring above the 30-day moving average remain the most profitable group in which to take a long position.

Now consider up gaps by looking at the results presented in Table 7.6. The sample contains 116,903 up gaps with the vast majority occurring above the average price. Eighty-nine percent of the up gaps occur above the 10-day moving average. Even 61% of the gaps meet the more stringent requirement of occurring above all three moving averages. Thirty-one percent of up gaps occur below the 90-day moving average, but of these gaps, approximately 79% occur at a price that is above the 10-day and the 30-day moving averages.

TABLE 7.6 Returns for Up Gaps Occurring Below and Above Multiple Price Moving Averages

		Gap Size	Number of Occurrences	Returns					Market-Adjusted Returns				
				1-day	3-day	5-day	10-day	30-day	1-day	3-day	5-day	10-day	30-day
All Up Gaps		1.1052	116,903	-0.0903	-0.1802	-0.0229	-0.0474	0.9449	-0.0588	-0.1110	-0.0337	-0.0483	0.3631
Below Moving Average	10-day SMA	0.7913	13,204	-0.3460	-0.2253	-0.0619	-0.2377	1.8713	-0.2074	-0.1416	-0.0828	-0.1500	0.6381
	30-day SMA	0.9418	27,532	-0.2662	-0.3018	-0.2391	-0.4847	1.1360	-0.1659	-0.2326	-0.2247	-0.4474	0.1895
	90-day SMA	1.0760	35,810	-0.1933	-0.3503	-0.1989	-0.3162	0.7045	-0.0988	-0.1770	-0.1054	-0.2205	0.1734
	10/30 combo	0.8484	10,309	-0.4160	-0.3043	-0.1043	-0.3110	1.9887	-0.2460	-0.2066	-0.1428	-0.2353	0.6614
	10/90 combo	0.9014	8,175	-0.5410	-0.4333	-0.1987	-0.3950	1.9029	-0.2895	-0.1798	-0.0895	-0.2308	0.6630
	10/30/90 combo	0.9199	7,623	-0.5603	-0.4441	-0.1911	-0.4066	1.9183	-0.3064	-0.2009	-0.1045	-0.2598	0.6554
Above Moving Average	10-day SMA	1.1447	103,604	-0.0566	-0.1729	-0.0150	-0.0214	0.8310	-0.0388	-0.1055	-0.0246	-0.0337	0.3314
	30-day SMA	1.1540	89,054	-0.0358	-0.1409	0.0502	0.0920	0.8822	-0.0258	-0.0720	0.0310	0.0791	0.4110
	90-day SMA	1.1126	80,204	-0.0467	-0.1029	0.0677	0.0739	1.0317	-0.0436	-0.0802	0.0084	0.0297	0.4230
	10/30 combo	1.1732	86,182	-0.0337	-0.1484	0.0472	0.0922	0.8632	-0.0242	-0.0781	0.0261	0.0747	0.4066
	10/90 combo	1.1461	75,265	-0.0483	-0.1213	0.0555	0.0725	0.9770	-0.0418	-0.0839	0.0086	0.0285	0.4098
	10/30/90 combo	1.1669	71,111	-0.0443	-0.1234	0.0677	0.0854	0.9357	-0.0390	-0.0778	0.0277	0.0609	0.4204

Although Table 7.6 gives some additional information of the incidence of up gaps occurring at relatively high and low prices, it unfortunately does not give much additional information regarding the profitability of potential trading strategies. You have repeatedly seen that up gaps are followed by negative 1-day and 3-day returns. Refining the classification a bit more doesn't alter those results. You also don't see a pattern of a different magnitude of returns when you combine two or three moving averages.

Summary

This chapter focused on the impact the price at which a gap occurs relative to the average price for the stock has on the profitability of trading strategies. Most up gaps occur at above average prices, and most down gaps occur at below average prices. The vast majority of gaps occur within a 75% to 125% range of the stock's price moving average. Some gaps, however, do occur at extremely high and extremely low price levels.

A consistent result throughout this chapter has been that stocks that gap down at above average prices tend to reverse price direction immediately. This suggests that purchasing a stock that gapped down on Day 0 at an above average price at the opening the following day, Day 1, will, on average, be a profitable trading strategy.

Stocks that gap up tend to have negative returns immediately following the gap. These negative returns tend to occur for a longer period of time for the stocks that gap up at relatively low prices. Stocks that gap up at a price below their 10-day, 30-day, or 90-day moving average still have negative returns at the 10-day holding period. By the 30-day mark, these returns have become positive.

Endnotes

1. Kirkpatrick, Charles and Julie Dahlquist. Technical Analysis: *The Complete Resource for Financial Market Technicians.* Upper Saddle River, NJ: Pearson Education, Inc., 2011.

2. On the rare occasion that the current price was exactly equal to the moving average, the current price was classified as above the moving average. This happened occasionally when using a 10-day moving average but was much less frequent when using the longer 30-day and 90-day moving averages. The number of observations gapping above and below a given length moving average does not always sum to the total number of gaps observed because some gaps occurred when a stock was newly included in the database and did not have enough previous price data to calculate a moving average.

Chapter 8

Gaps and the Market

This chapter analyzes gaps in relation to overall market movement. Some days have an extremely high number of gaps. The gaps on these high gap days are tipped heavily in one direction. For example, there might be 599 gaps on one day, with all but 3 of them being up gaps. Does this situation point you toward certain trading strategies? Does it give you a clue as to which direction the market might be headed? A different question related to market movements is: Should prior market movements alter your interpretation of individual stock gaps? For example, is there a difference in how you might interpret a gap down for a stock if the market is already trending down? These are some of the questions this chapter explores.

High Gap Days

First consider the issue of the total number of gaps occurring in the market on a given day. The total number of gaps in a given day can vary greatly. The distribution is not uniform across time. On some days, more than 500 stocks gap. Of those 500, all might be down gaps. Or the vast majority may be down gaps. The same is true for up gaps. Do these dominant direction high gap days give you any clue about future market direction?

Table 8.1 shows the 25 days in our study that had the most total gaps. The table shows the date, total gaps, the breakdown of down versus up gaps, and the average size of the gaps. As can be seen, there were 25 days on which 553 or more gaps occurred. Nine of those days had gaps only in one direction. The remaining 16 days had less than 10 gaps in the opposite direction from the majority. You might expect to see such a one-sided split if the average gap size were quite large, but that is not the case. For example, on December 1, 2010, the average gap up size was only 0.576%, but there were 617 up gaps and only six stocks that gapped down. The largest average gap in this list for the majority side was –1.781% on September 22, 2011.

In looking at the list, something striking jumps out. Fourteen of the 25 days with the largest number of gaps occurred in 2011. Actually, nine of the top ten in the list occurred in 2011; furthermore, these nine occurred during the months of September–November 2011. This raises some interesting questions. In Chapter 3, "The Occurrence of Gaps," you saw that the total number of gaps in a year has been rising steadily. So is the fact that so many of the high gap days occurred in 2011 just a consequence of increased gap activity over time? Digging further, you can see that the earliest date in the list is February 27, 2007. That gaps have been occurring more frequently over time is a factor, however it goes beyond that simple explanation; 2011 was an especially turbulent year in several respects.

TABLE 8.1 *Days with the Greatest Number of Gaps*

	Date	Total Gaps	Gaps Down	Gaps Up	Average Gap Down Size	Average Gap Up Size
1	8/18/2011	1,277	1,276	1	-1.6682	0.9610
2	9/22/2011	1,160	1,159	1	-1.7814	7.4373
3	11/30/2011	1,066	1	1,065	-1.9892	1.4837
4	9/7/2011	1,040	3	1,037	-0.5153	0.9098
5	9/2/2011	1,032	1,025	7	-1.0513	0.6688
6	8/29/2011	958	—	958	—	0.6915
7	11/1/2011	951	949	2	-1.3732	4.0507
8	10/27/2011	891	9	882	-6.8063	1.5247
9	9/27/2011	808	1	807	-3.1111	1.0838
10	6/29/2010	784	784	—	-0.9092	—
11	8/11/2010	711	711	—	-0.7734	—
12	10/6/2008	706	706	—	-1.5658	—
13	2/17/2009	653	649	4	-1.5132	6.9980
14	11/21/2011	645	644	1	-0.7753	1.2607
15	4/2/2009	627	—	627	—	1.3819

(continues)

TABLE 8.1   *Days with the Greatest Number of Gaps (continued)*

	Date	Total Gaps	Gaps Down	Gaps Up	Average Gap Down Size	Average Gap Up Size
16	11/28/2011	627	1	626	−0.1928	0.9527
17	12/1/2010	623	6	617	−4.6514	0.5757
18	4/20/2011	599	3	596	−0.7054	0.8273
19	3/30/2009	582	582	—	−1.3403	—
20	5/23/2011	579	579	—	−0.5857	—
21	2/27/2007	566	563	3	−0.7549	1.6290
22	9/6/2011	563	562	1	−0.8498	20.7129
23	8/24/2010	554	554	—	−0.7128	—
24	6/1/2009	553	—	553	—	0.9404
25	4/9/2009	553	4	549	−2.6201	1.3142

One way that market volatility is measured is the VIX. The VIX is an index of volatility for the S&P 500 index. Figure 8.1 shows a graph of the VIX over the 2005–2011 time period. During this period the value of the VIX exceeded a level of 40 during three subperiods: October 2008–April 2009, May–July 2010, and August–October 2011. Twelve of the 25 days with the largest number of gaps in Table 8.1 occurred during these three subperiods; 7 of those days (about one-third of the high gap days) occurred during the August–October 2011 period.

However, just looking at the VIX doesn't tell you what is behind the volatility; it simply measures the volatility. To investigate at a deeper level what might be behind the price movement on these particular days, consider the news on these 25 days. A summary of events occurring on those days is provided on the following pages.

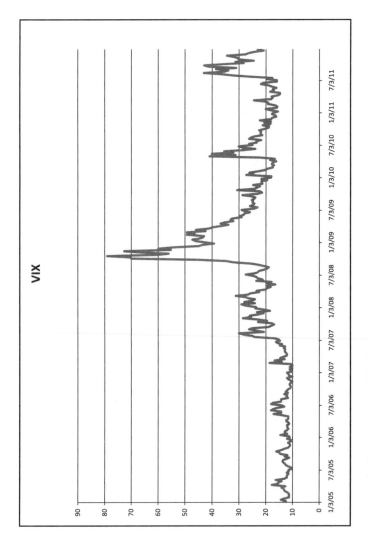

FIGURE 8.1   *Volatility as measured by the VIX, 2005–2011*

Major News Events on High Gap Days

What was occurring that may have caused so many gaps to occur on particular days? Remember that it is new, unexpected news and information that market participants receive that can cause a jump in price. In addition, for gaps to occur, this news is usually information that becomes available after the close of one trading session but before the open of the next session. To highlight the development of news and events on these days with a high number of gaps, the news summaries are in chronological order:

Tuesday, February 27, 2007
(563 down gaps/3 up gaps)

The U.S. markets opened on the heels of the Chinese (Shanghai) market dropping 8.8% overnight, the largest drop in a decade, on worries that the Chinese government was going to take actions to reduce the amount of stock speculation. In addition to the negative impact of the news from China, a decline in durable goods orders raised concerns about the U.S. economy. Investors were also mulling over comments made on the previous day by former Federal Reserve Board Chairman Alan Greenspan that he thought the U.S. economy might enter a recession at the end of the year. And if those factors were not enough to create a turbulent day, Vice-President Dick Cheney had been the apparent target that day of a Taliban suicide mission in Afghanistan that killed 23 people. (Cheney was unhurt.)

Monday, October 6, 2008
(706 down gaps/0 up gaps)

Concerns over bank bailout plans in the United States and problems in European banks caused the Dow to drop as much as 800 points during the day. Interestingly, Jim Cramer (of *Mad Money* fame) was interviewed on the *Today* show and advised people to take all the money they might need for the next 5 years out of the stock market.

Tuesday, February 17, 2009
(649 down gaps/4 up gaps)

Obama signed the $787 billion American Recovery and Reinvestment Act into law. The market continued to worry about U.S. banks, problems with GM and Chrysler, and a worsening recession in Japan.

Monday, March 30, 2009
(582 down gaps/0 up gaps)

The market fell on concerns over GM, Chrysler, and bank stocks. The Obama administration said that GM and Chrysler had one more attempt at restructuring. In addition, many banks were probably going to need substantial federal aid.

Thursday, April 2, 2009
(0 down gaps/627 up gaps)

The market jumped up with news of a coordinated effort among central banks to prop up financial markets.

Thursday, April 9, 2009
(4 down gaps/549 up gaps)

The market moved up as Wells Fargo issued a brighter earnings outlook. Oil prices moved up following the stock market's rise.

Monday, June 1, 2009
(0 down gaps/553 up gaps)

Markets moved higher after a report on manufacturing showed that activity was declining less than expected. Sometimes what seems like bad news can be good news, if the market is expecting something worse than what actually happens. In other news, GM and Citigroup were replaced by Cisco and The Travelers Companies in the Dow Jones Industrial Average.

Tuesday, June 29, 2010
(784 down gaps/0 up gaps)

Markets dropped with the news that the Consumer Confidence Index had fallen. There were also concerns about the economies of Japan, China, and Greece.

Wednesday, August 11, 2010
(711 down gaps/0 up gaps)

A report on a growing U.S. trade gap raised concerns that foreign demand for U.S. goods was diminishing. In addition, there was news that heightened concerns about the UK and Chinese economies.

Tuesday, August 24, 2010
(554 down gaps/0 up gaps)

A worse than expected drop in existing home sales caused stocks to fall. Many investors still had major concerns about the U.S. economy.

Wednesday, December 1, 2010
(6 down gaps/617 up gaps)

Positive news about employment data and auto sales lifted the market.

Wednesday, April 20, 2011
(3 down gaps/596 up gaps)

Strong earnings in the technology sector boosted the market.

Monday, May 23, 2011
(579 down gaps/0 up gaps)

Investors became increasingly nervous after rating agencies downgraded the debt of Greece and Italy. On the domestic front, earnings from retailers were disappointing.

Thursday, August 18, 2011
(1277 down gaps/1 up gap)

There were more down gaps on this date than any other day in the study. The Dow Jones Industrial Average dropped more than 400 points on fears about the global economy in general and the health of European banks. On the domestic front, news concerning manufacturing activity, jobless claims, consumer prices, and existing home sales was all negative.

Monday, August 29, 2011
(0 down gaps/958 up gaps)

No news can be good news. The northeastern United States had been bracing for Hurricane Irene, but damage was far less than had been feared.

Friday, September 2, 2011
(1025 down gaps/7 up gaps)

Fear that the U.S. economy would dip back into recession grew as the Labor Department reported a zero rate of job growth for August. The DJIA fell 2.2% and the S&P500 index fell 2.5%, leading into the 3-day Labor Day weekend.

Tuesday, September 6, 2011
(562 down gaps/ 1 up gap)

Due to Labor Day, the market was closed on Monday, a day of major selling in Europe. When U.S. markets opened on Tuesday, the 6th, the sell-off hit the United States. With the worsening situation in Greece and Italy investors were becoming increasingly worried about the economies of many European countries.

Wednesday, September 7, 2011
(3 down gaps/1037 up gaps)

A major court ruling in Germany buoyed optimism that Angela Merkel could help engineer a European bailout for Europe's struggling economies. After 2 consecutive trading days with an unusually large number of down gaps, the market reversed with an unusually high number of up gaps occurring.

Thursday, September 22, 2011
(1159 down gaps/1 up gap)

The market reacted negatively to a 2-day policy meeting of the Fed. Concerns about the U.S. economy and the situation in Europe remained high. In addition, growth in China appeared to be slowing.

Tuesday, September 27, 2011
(1 down gap/807 up gaps)

The market rallied as European officials were reported to be working on a detailed plan to shore up the stability of European banks.

Thursday, October 27, 2011
(9 down gaps/882 up gaps)

Investors reacted positively to the news that the EU was increasing its bailout fund and was willing to take major losses on Greek bonds.

Tuesday, November 1, 2011
(949 down gaps/2 up gaps)

Markets were jolted by Greece's surprising decision to hold a referendum on a European rescue package.

Monday, November 21, 2011
(644 down gaps/1 up gap)

Political inaction on both sides of the Atlantic worried investors. They were frustrated with the lack of progress in Europe concerning the Eurozone crisis and with the failure of the Congressional "supercommittee" to reach a deal over budget deficit cuts.

Monday, November 28, 2011
(1 down gap/626 up gaps)

Stronger than expected Black Friday sales by retailers and an increase in new home sales boosted optimism in the market.

Wednesday, November 30, 2011
(1 down gap/1065 up gaps)

Stocks rallied on news that the world's top central banks were coordinating efforts to help the global economy.

There is an old maxim that says "what goes around comes around." The Austrian statesman Prince Metternich once said "When Paris sneezes, Europe catches a cold"—or at least something quite similar. (There is some dispute about the exact quote.) This quote was later altered by many to be "When the U.S.

sneezes, the world catches a cold." However, looking at the preceding international relationships, something such as "When Europe or Asia sneezes, the United States catches a cold" may now be more appropriate.

Looking at the high gap days chronologically highlights the clustering of these days within the August through November 2011 time period. Figure 8.3 shows that four of these high gap days occurred within the 7-day trading period of August 29–September 7, 2011. Monday, August 29, was a high up gap day and the S&P500 index rose. On each of the following 2 days, the S&P500 index rose slightly. Thursday's decline in the S&P500 erased those gains. Then, on Friday, September 2, a high gap down day occurred. The S&P500 dropped, more than erasing Monday's gains, leaving the S&P500 down slightly for the week. The next 3 days were Labor Day weekend, so Tuesday, September 6, was the next trading day. On Tuesday the S&P500 experienced another down move and 562 stocks gapped down. After 2 consecutive high down gap trading days, a high up gap day occurred on Wednesday, September 7.

You might think that 4 high gap trading days clustered so close together would indicate some major movement in the market. However, Figure 8.1 tells a different story. The S&P500 dropped approximately 14% over the July 25–August 8 time frame and then entered a congestion area. The frequent high gap days were representative of market indecision and the battle between buyers and sellers was more than a push of the market in a particular direction.

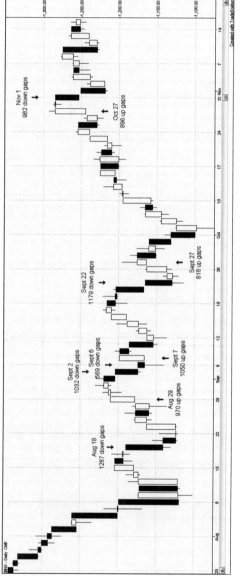

FIGURE 8.2   Daily chart for the S&P500 Index, July 25–November 15, 2011

On days with a large number of gaps, it would seem reasonable that there might also have been gaps in some of the major market indexes. However, that is not necessarily the case. Figure 8.2 shows the behavior of the S&P 500 Index and SPY over the latter part of 2011. The chart shows many examples of gaps in SPY, but the index itself only gapped on 2 days: September 22, 2011 and November 1, 2011. The S&P 500 ETF (ticker SPY) tracks the S&P. This shows that sometimes even with gaps in a large proportion of the index component stocks, the index or index-based ETF may not gap.

Trading High Gap Days

What types of trading opportunities might these large gap days present? Three possible approaches are discussed. First, high gap days might provide some type of market timing signal. For example, if an investor observed a large number of up gaps on a given day, he might buy shares of SPY, with the hope that the S&P 500 Index was headed up. This would be taking a **continuation approach**. Alternatively, he could sell SPY, counting on a reversal. With either approach the investor would be looking to the large number of gaps as a signal regarding future market direction. A second approach would be to buy or sell some of the stocks that were part of the group of stocks gapping in the same direction. This could be done either with a continuation or a **reversal** outlook, so it would be similar to the first approach, but trading the individual stocks rather than an index-based ETF. A third approach would be to buy or sell the few stocks that gapped in the **opposite** direction from the pack. If 562 stocks gapped down and only one gapped up, surely there is something unusual with that stock that may or may not present a trading opportunity. Now examine all three possible approaches.

Begin by examining the first approach, which uses the high gap days as a market timing signal. Table 8.2 shows the returns on SPY, the S&P 500-based ETF, over various subsequent periods. These returns were calculated using the same basic procedure as that used for individual stock gaps. The *n*-day return assumes that SPY was purchased at the opening price on the day after the gap and then sold at the close on day *n*. It appears that these high gap days do not necessarily provide useful trading signals. Furthermore, that is true whether you consider a continuation approach or a reversal approach.

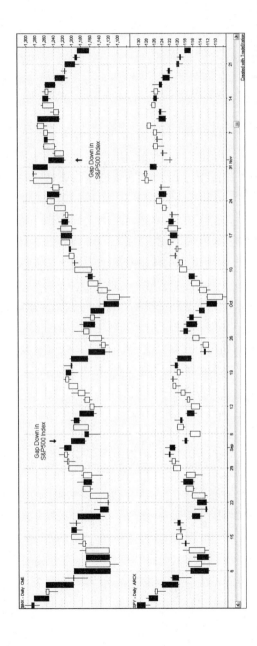

FIGURE 8.3   *Daily chart for the S&P500 Index ($INX) and SPY, August 1–November 23, 2011*

Created with TradeStation

TABLE 8.2   *Returns on SPY after High Gap Days*

Date	Gap Size	Total	Down	Up	SPY 1-Day	SPY 3-Day	SPY 5-Day	SPY 10-Day	SPY 30-Day
8/18/2011	-1.6662	1,277	1,276	1	-0.2833	3.0811	2.9410	7.0648	0.1733
9/22/2011	-1.7734	1,160	1,159	1	1.2755	4.8435	3.5144	3.9069	12.6126
11/30/2011	1.4805	1,066	1	1,065	0.0961	1.0973	1.5058	-2.4910	3.1958
9/7/2011	0.9057	1,040	3	1,037	-0.4433	-2.4254	-0.1673	-2.4588	1.3047
9/2/2011	-1.0396	1,032	1,025	7	2.2729	4.0650	1.9932	5.1753	5.1053
8/29/2011	0.6915	958	—	958	0.7035	0.0910	-3.1780	-2.5573	-0.9352
11/1/2011	-1.3618	951	949	2	0.1292	1.3325	3.2706	1.8170	-1.6874
10/27/2011	1.4406	891	9	882	0.4688	-4.6875	-1.3672	-2.8750	-1.5234
9/27/2011	1.0786	808	1	807	-2.2415	-3.9311	-4.6188	1.6302	8.5753
6/29/2010	-0.9092	784	784	—	-0.6736	-1.6551	2.1074	5.5139	5.1758
8/11/2010	-0.7734	711	711	—	0.9104	0.5667	1.9879	-1.5885	4.5053
10/6/2008	-1.5658	706	706	—	-6.3740	-15.1067	-5.1385	-7.5159	-20.0019
2/17/2009	-1.4611	653	649	4	-0.9525	-2.9703	-2.8951	-12.1820	-0.3384
11/21/2011	-0.7722	645	644	1	-0.1759	-2.5628	0.5444	5.7454	7.2362
4/2/2009	1.3819	627	—	627	0.9223	-2.2039	2.7788	4.2999	6.2522
11/28/2011	0.9509	627	1	626	0.0000	4.0983	5.1395	3.4652	7.6218
12/1/2010	0.5254	623	6	617	1.1221	1.2871	1.7162	2.3927	5.9158

Date	Gap Size	Total	Down	Up	SPY 1-Day	SPY 3-Day	SPY 5-Day	SPY 10-Day	SPY 30-Day
4/20/2011	0.8196	599	3	596	-0.0075	0.7474	1.7345	-0.1338	-2.5206
3/30/2009	-1.3403	582	582	—	-0.0503	4.8643	5.0779	6.0206	14.3414
5/23/2011	-0.5857	579	579	—	-0.3700	0.4228	1.8574	-2.6276	1.1552
2/27/2007	-0.7422	566	563	3	0.3846	-1.2252	-0.4915	-1.5243	2.5865
9/6/2011	-0.8115	563	562	1	1.2883	-2.3914	-0.8589	1.1873	3.2166
8/24/2010	-0.7128	554	554	—	0.9433	1.8199	0.3430	5.2025	10.5574
6/1/2009	0.9404	553	—	553	0.4767	0.1377	-0.2542	-1.5890	-4.0148
4/9/2009	1.2857	553	4	549	1.0716	0.3886	2.5436	2.0490	4.8281

A reversal approach would have worked well using a 5-day holding period immediately after the gap date for the 6 days with the largest number of down gaps. The 5-day returns for these gaps (8/18/11, 9/22/11, 9/2/11, 11/1/11, 6/29/10, and 8/11/10) were 2.94%, 3.51%, 1.99%, 3.27%, 2.11%, and 1.99%, respectively. However, the 5-day return following the 10/6/08 gap, which was the day with the next highest number of gaps, was −5.14% (the 3-day return was −15.11%). There were 14 high down gap days in Table 8.2. The average 5-day return for a reversal strategy following these 14 days was 1.02%, which is quite good. In addition, the return was positive for 10 of the 14 instances. These results might lead you to the idea that a reversal strategy following the high gap days would be the way to approach things.

However, looking at the 11 days with a high number of up gaps might make you pause. The average 5-day return for a reversal strategy in this case would have been −0.53%. A reversal strategy (using a 5-day holding period) would have been profitable for only 4 out of the 11 instances. What if you took a long position after every high gap day, regardless of gap direction? The average 5-day return was 0.80%, which annualized is more than 40%. However, ignoring the gap direction seems rather odd. Twenty-five observations is not a big sample and the variability in the results is quite high.

Is there any reliable strategy for using these high gap days to time the market as a whole? If there is, the authors didn't see it. But, that certainly doesn't mean that it's not there. The high gap days are definitely intriguing. Intuitively you would think that they must contain some valuable information about future market direction.

A second approach would be to buy or sell some of the individual stocks that are part of the large group of stocks gapping in the same direction. Table 8.3 addresses this approach. First consider the days with a high number of down gaps. The 1-day return (both unadjusted and market-adjusted) is negative for the stocks that gapped down. But, the 3, 5, 10, and 30 returns are all positive. The trading idea would be to perhaps go short on the down-gapping stocks on the day after the gap, looking for a downward continuation. But, after Day 1 it appears that it would be better to be long, hoping for a reversal. The magnitude of the returns is quite high, which is certainly intriguing.

In Table 8.4 most of the stocks are gapping up. Here a possible trading strategy is not as clear. On the day after the gap, it looks like a continuation strategy would be best because the 1-day returns on the up-gapping stocks are positive. But, after Day 1 the stocks, on average, reverse direction, which would mean switching to a reversal strategy. For the down gap strategy, all the returns after Day 1 were the same sign, positive. However, that is not true for the up gaps. Some of the 5-, 10-, and 30-day returns are positive and some are negative. The reversal approach looks attractive between Days 1 and 3, but past that it's hard to say.

TABLE 8.3   Returns for Stocks That Gap on High Down Gap Days

Gap Size	Number of Occurrences	Returns					Market-Adjusted Returns				
		1-day	3-day	5-day	10-day	30-day	1-day	3-day	5-day	10-day	30-day
Down Gaps	-1.1952	10,743	-0.1113	0.4836	1.4935	2.1935	3.5184	-0.0812	0.3078	0.1584	0.4317	0.3369
Up Gaps	3.8017	20	-0.7354	-1.3340	-2.4479	-5.1118	-4.3379	-1.5163	-2.2607	-3.1267	-5.3350	-7.4378

TABLE 8.4   Returns for Stocks That Gap on High Up Gap Days

Gap Size	Number of Occurrences	Returns					Market-Adjusted Returns				
		1-day	3-day	5-day	10-day	30-day	1-day	3-day	5-day	10-day	30-day
Down Gaps	-3.8786	28	-0.1113	-0.9020	1.3635	1.3271	2.2780	-0.5306	0.4080	0.8315	1.6306	0.2478
Up Gaps	1.0771	8,317	0.1807	-1.0191	0.4156	-0.4530	2.6243	0.0557	-0.3154	0.2039	-0.1687	0.1346

A third approach is to trade the stocks that are gap-ping in the opposite direction. Surely there must be something unusual about that stock or small group of stocks. To examine this possibility dig into the details of the stocks in Table 8.3 that fought the herd. The returns for the stocks that gapped up when almost all the rest were gapping down are quite intriguing. All ten return numbers across the row are negative and the returns increase in magnitude as the holding period increases. A reversal strategy, going short on the stocks that gap, looks attractive. But the sample size is small; there are only 20 observations.

Looking at the down-gapping stocks, when large numbers are gapping up, the returns (refer to Table 8.4) for the first few days are negative. After Day 3 though, they turn positive. This would suggest that initially a continuation strategy might be best, but that price may reverse direction fairly soon. The sample size here is still small, only 28.

The number of stocks bucking the trend on the high gap days is small, but the stocks appear to present inter-esting trading opportunities when they do occur. It can be worthwhile to drill down to a deeper level, trying to understand what happens in these situations. Therefore, consider some of the specific circumstances concerning the stocks that move counter to the rest of the pack on high gap days.

Only one stock gapped up on August 18, 2011 whereas 1,276 gapped down: Central Gold Trust (GTU), which is a Canadian company that invests pri-marily in gold bullion. As you just saw, not only did a record number of stocks gap down on August 18, but also the DJIA dropped more than 400 points amid global economic concerns. Because many investors turn to gold—wanting hard assets rather than financial assets—when they are nervous, it makes sense that this stock had a good day on August 18. As shown in Figure 8.4, GTU continued moving up during part of the day on the 19th but closed down on the 19th and the following 3 trading days (August 22, 23, and 24). As part of its downward move, GTU had a large down gap on August 23. How did GTU's move compare to the overall market those next few days? SPY continued moving down on August 19 and 22 but turned up fairly strongly on the 23rd, closing higher on the 23rd and 24th.

On September 22, 2011, only one stock gapped up, swimming against the tide as 1,179 stocks gapped down. The stock was Goodrich Corporation (GR), which is in the aerospace/defense industry. Here, as you can see in Figure 8.5, the story actually begins before September 22. On September 16, GR moved up more than 7% on rumors (that were reported in *The New York Times* that evening) that the company might be taken over by United Technologies. Over the next 3 days (September 19, 20, and 21), it continued to move up, rising from a close of 92.89 on the September 16 to a close of 109.49 on September 21. The large gap up (7.44%) on September 22 was driven by the announcement that United Technologies had agreed to buy GR. It closed at 120.60 on September 22 and finished the year at $123.70.

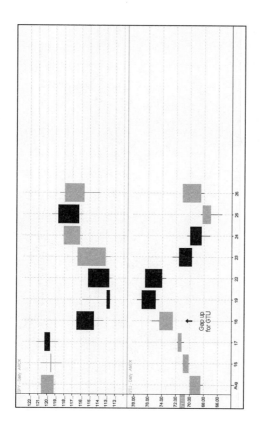

FIGURE 8.4   *Daily chart of GTU and SPY, August 15–24, 2011*

Created with TradeStation

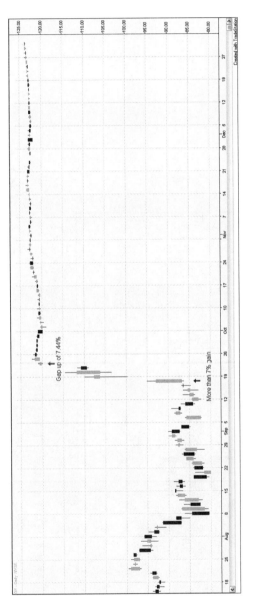

FIGURE 8.5   Daily stock chart for GR, August 13–December 31, 2011

Omnivision Technologies, Inc. (OVTI) was the only stock that gapped down on November 30, 2011. The drop followed the release of its latest quarterly financials, which the market found disappointing. The same thing had happened the previous quarter when the stock gapped down on August 26, resulting in a price drop of 30% in one day. You can see in Figure 8.6 that OVTI's high was slightly more than 35 on July 1. On November 30, the low for the day was 10.15, quite a drop in just five months. The 5-day return after November 30 was 18.4%. There was a good opportunity to make money by betting on a short-term reversal and going long OVTI at the open on Thursday, December 1, but the opportunity probably would have been difficult to foresee.

The three stocks that gapped down on September 7, 2011 (Darden Restaurant [DRI], Frontier Communication [FTR], and Novagold Resources [NG]) all continued moving down the following day. The 10-day return on all three was negative, but DRI and FTR did come back up some before continuing down. The best of the three to short would have been NG. Looking at Figure 8.7, the day of the gap was not a huge attention getter by itself. However, consider the context in which this gap occurred. The two previous trading days, September 2 and September 6, NG had two relatively tall white candles. Remember that those two trading days were number 3 and number 13, respectively, on a list of days with the largest number of down gaps. Thus, NG's rise on September 2 and 6 occurred against an extremely bearish market background. Then, on September 7, the market moved higher with 1,037 gap ups, the second largest number in the study. As one of only three stocks that gapped down that day, NG was definitely swimming against the tide.

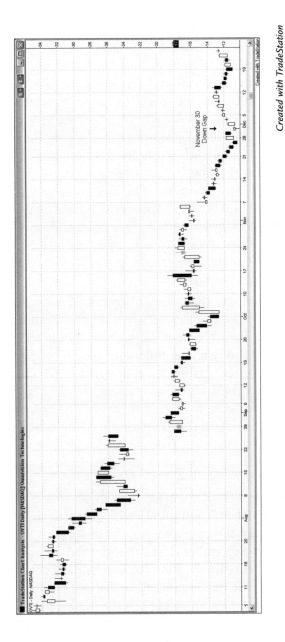

Created with TradeStation

FIGURE 8.6   *Daily stock chart for OTVI, July 1–December 23, 2011*

A trader shorting NG at the open on September 8 would have enjoyed a nice profit as the stock continued down, punching through support at about 8.60. The 10-day return would have been 28.77%. On Day 11, another gap down occurred, and a short position would have continued to be profitable as the stock dropped steadily, finally bottoming just below 6 on October 4.

Unlike NG, FTR fell on September 2 and September 6 along with the broader market. Instead of rebounding on September 7 as much of the rest of the market did, however, FTR gapped down. An investor who, thinking this downtrend would continue, went short at the open on September 8, would have had a profit by Day 10. As shown in Figure 8.8, FTR continued in a downtrend through the end of 2011.

The third stock to gap down on September 7, DRI (see Figure 8.9), had also fallen the two previous days along with the broader market. DRI was one of the 1,025 stocks that gapped down on September 2. Unlike the broader market, DRI did not recover on September 7; instead it gapped down again. Investors who shorted DRI at the open on September 8 would have positive 1-, 3-, 5-, and 10-day returns, although the stock was in a trading range for the rest of 2011.

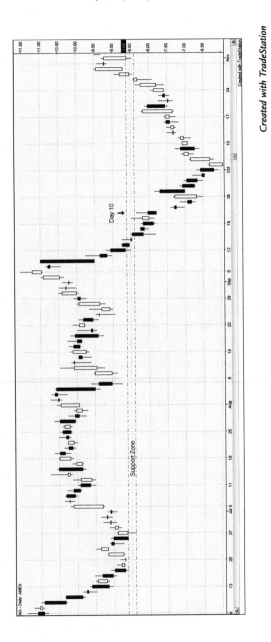

FIGURE 8.7   *Daily stock chart for NG, June 6–November 1, 2011*

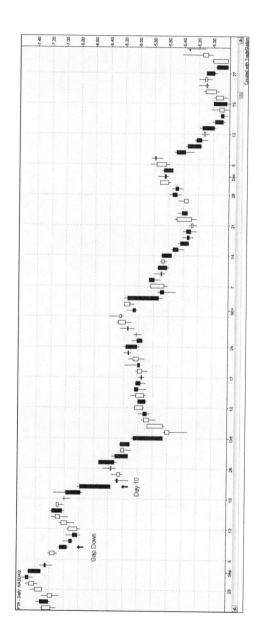

FIGURE 8.8 *Daily stock chart for FTR, September 24–December 31, 2011*

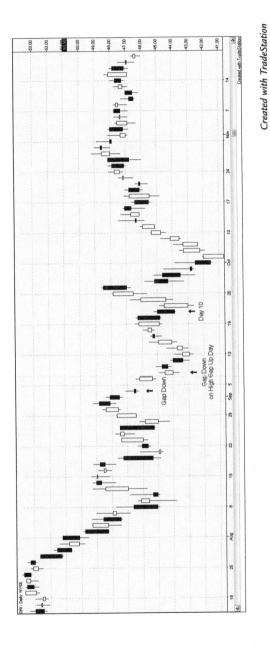

FIGURE 8.9   *Daily stock chart for DRI, July 13–November 18, 2011*

September 2, 2011 was an interesting day. Seven stocks gapped up that day whereas 1,025 went the other direction. The seven were Endeavour Silver Corporation (EXK), Finisar Corporation (FNSR), MineFinders Corporation (MFN), Newmont Mining Corporation (NEM), Sprott Physical Silver Trust (PSLV), Royal Gold Inc. (RGLD), and Silver Wheaton Corporation (SLW). Six of the seven stocks are related to gold or silver in some manner. The short term price behavior of this group was not consistent; however the average 30-day return was −16.89%. Because the market went up some over that same period, the adjusted return of −21.99% was even better (for those in a short position). These results suggest that precious metal stocks may warrant special attention on days with a high number of gaps.

There were only two stocks that gapped up on November 1, 2011, whereas almost a thousand gapped down. The case of ITT Corporation (ITT) on that day was unusual. Reverse splits are not too common, but ITT underwent a 1:2 reverse split on that day. In addition to the split, ITT shareholders of record as of October 17 also received one share of Exelis Inc. (XLS) and one share of Xylem Inc. (XLY) on October 31. The ex-distribution date for the distribution and the reverse split was November 1. The two other stocks that gapped up on the November 1 were Leap Wireless International Inc. (LEAP) and (VRUS).

We have discussed the specific stocks that for the seven days with the highest number of gaps were gapping counter to the crowd, going through things day by day. What are some of the common factors that caused stocks to go in the opposite direction from the rest of the crowd?

One common cause for gaps is reaction to earnings reports. On October 27, 2011, only 9 stocks gapped down whereas 882 gapped up. Of the 9 stocks gapping down, 8 of the gaps were negative reactions to earnings reports. Similarly, on April 20, 2011, only 3 stocks gapped down, all on disappointing earnings reports.

Many gaps are related to merger and acquisition activity, as previously discussed in Chapter 3. A good example of how a stock's price may exhibit some wild gyrations around a hostile takeover bid occurred during June–September, 2011, with Temple-Inland (TIN). On September 6, 2011, while 562 stocks gapped down that day, Temple-Inland (TIN) was the lone stock to gap up. News that International Paper had finally reached an agreement with Temple-Inland after increasing its previous bid to $32 per share sent the shares up by about 25% to a close of 30.85. However, the fireworks had started earlier. TIN had previously gapped up by approximately 40% to near $30 on June 7. The news that drove that upward price jump was unusual. TIN had adopted a poison pill defense in an attempt to fend off a hostile takeover by International Paper. On August 18, TIN gapped down along with 1,286 other stocks, losing approximately 7% of its value. That move took the price back down below $26. But another big down gap was still just slightly up ahead. On August 23, TIN dropped another 14%, closing at 21.33. The price even went as low as 19.03 at one point during that day. This drop in price came from another direction. TIN was sued over the 2009 failure of a Texas bank that it had spun off in 2007. So in the space of just 3 months, TIN had experienced two up gaps, each more than 25%, and two down gaps, each more than 7%.

There is plenty of evidence that the market usually reacts negatively whenever a company issues more stock. On September 27, 2011, Coffee Holding Company (JVA) gapped down and closed down by 15.6% whereas 807 other stocks gapped up. JVA had moved down in response to an announcement that the company had entered into an agreement with some institutional investors to sell 890,000 units that consisted of one share of common stock per unit and three-tenths of a warrant for one share of common stock. Similarly, on April 9, 2009, the market reacted negatively to Equity One's (EQY) announcement that it was selling additional stock to raise cash. The market also did not like Omnicare's (OCR) announcement on December 1, 2010, that it was raising money by issuing some Convertible Senior Secured Notes. This caused the stock to gap down, closing down by 3.6% (issuing notes is less distasteful to investors), whereas 617 other stocks gapped up.

Most of the events that caused some stocks to move opposite to the pack on the 25 days with the largest number of gaps have been discussed. As you saw, there is usually some significant piece of news that is the cause. Now return to the question: Do stocks that go against the rest of the herd offer tradable opportunities? In general, probably not. Although there are certain common causes (earnings announcements, takeovers, issuance of securities, and so on) each case is unique. Price moves subsequent to the gaps can be large. The overall averages in Tables 8.3 and 8.4 look intriguing, but approach with caution. These types of gaps probably warrant investigation on a case by case basis.

Market Movements and Gap Trading

Next turn to a different question: Should market movements influence your individual stock gap-based trading decisions? For example, assume that the market has been in a strong uptrend and you are considering whether to go long or short with stocks that have gapped up. Do you go long, staying with the stock's upward movement and the market's upward movement, or do you perhaps look for a reversal?

Using the same SPDR S&P 500 (SPY) price data we used to calculate market-adjusted returns, we calculate 1-, 3-, 5-, 10-, 30-, and 90-day returns for each trading day from January 1, 1995, to December 31, 2011. To calculate the 3-day return, we first subtracted the closing price from Day −3 price for Day 0 and then divided that result by the closing price from Day −3. Similar calculations were done for the other time intervals. Also, we used data from the last 90 days in 1994 to calculate the 90-day (and other intervals) returns as of January 1, 1995. So for each day in our sample period, we had market returns for six different time periods ending on the day in question.

We then transformed the percentage returns into discrete categories somewhat along the lines of what we did with volume using two different approaches, which was discussed in Chapter 6, "Gaps and Volume." In the first approach, we categorized the market direction as either "up" or "down." For example, if the 5-day market return was positive (or zero, which occurs with very low frequency) the market was up for that period. If the return was negative, the market was down. So this variable associated with the 5-day return had only two possible values: up or down. Now consider the results from this approach before moving to the second approach.

Table 8.5 recaps the results for down gaps, whereas Table 8.6 recaps the results for the up gaps. The upper half of the table deals with the market moving down, whereas the lower half is for when the market moves up. The negative returns are shaded. At the simplest level of analysis, you can ask the same question for both tables: Does the pattern of shading look similar between the upper half of the table and the lower half? If prior market movement has an important impact on returns, you should see different patterns.

The shading patterns in the upper half of the table look similar to the shading patterns in the lower half for both tables. The shading pattern between the two tables is different; one table is for down gaps and the other is for up gaps. Therefore, gap direction does seem to make a difference. But, within each table separately, the top half appears to be similar to the bottom half. That would point toward the conclusion that prior market movement is irrelevant.

But there is a little more to the story, at least concerning down gaps. Look at the differences in the values between the upper half and lower half of each table. For the up gaps (Table 8.6) you don't see any particular pattern to the differences. But for the down gaps, the unadjusted returns are higher in 20 out of 25 cells for the market moving down (the upper half) section. Furthermore, the difference is quite substantial in many cases. For example, compare the 30-day returns for the market moving down over the last 3 days' row to the market moving up over the last 3 days' row; the numbers are 1.8049 and 0.1854, respectively. That is a difference of 1.6195%. Patterns are nice to have when investing. It would be nice if the market-adjusted returns showed a similar pattern, however they do not.

TABLE 8.5   Returns for Down Gaps When the Market Direction Is Down and Up

	Gap Size	Number of Occurrences	Returns					Market-Adjusted Returns				
			1-day	3-day	5-day	10-day	30-day	1-day	3-day	5-day	10-day	30-day
All Down Gaps	-1.3394	97,029	-0.0204	0.0198	0.3712	0.4793	1.3558	-0.0507	-0.0013	0.0478	0.1116	0.3783
Market Moving Down — 1 Day	-1.1856	71,995	-0.0164	0.0147	0.4578	0.6274	1.6403	-0.0885	-0.0426	-0.0009	0.0642	0.3334
3 day	-1.2011	70,123	0.0207	0.0608	0.5555	0.7349	1.8049	-0.0657	-0.0077	0.0659	0.1609	0.4618
5 Day	-1.2321	65,253	0.0237	0.2626	0.6474	0.7865	2.0559	-0.0403	0.0781	0.1080	0.1879	0.4977
10 Day	-1.2736	59,342	-0.0426	-0.0286	0.4886	0.5948	1.5526	-0.0829	-0.0300	0.0306	0.1726	0.3718
30 Day	-1.3405	49,464	-0.0514	-0.0498	0.4827	0.6485	1.6060	-0.0983	-0.0518	0.0287	0.1064	0.4720
90 Day	-1.4194	48,352	0.0518	0.1284	0.6509	0.7412	1.6116	-0.0795	0.0099	0.0559	0.1866	0.5654
Market Moving Up — 1 Day	-1.7815	25,034	-0.0318	0.0344	0.1222	0.0534	0.5376	0.0580	0.1173	0.1878	0.2481	0.5076
3 day	-1.6998	26,906	-0.1275	-0.0870	-0.1091	-0.1868	0.1854	-0.0116	0.0153	0.0006	-0.0168	0.1608
5 Day	-1.5598	31,776	-0.1109	-0.4788	-0.1959	-0.1516	-0.0820	-0.0721	-0.1644	-0.0759	-0.0449	0.1331
10 Day	-1.4430	37,687	0.0147	0.0961	0.1864	0.2973	1.0460	0.0000	0.0439	0.0749	0.0156	0.3885
30 Day	-1.3382	47,565	0.0119	0.0922	0.2552	0.3033	1.0956	-0.0013	0.0512	0.0676	0.1171	0.2809
90 Day	-1.2599	48,677	-0.0921	-0.0881	0.0934	0.2191	1.1017	-0.0221	-0.0124	0.0398	0.0372	0.1925

TABLE 8.6 Returns for Up Gaps When the Market Direction Is Down and Up

		Gap Size	Number of Occurrences	Returns					Market-Adjusted Returns				
				1-day	3-day	5-day	10-day	30-day	1-day	3-day	5-day	10-day	30-day
All Up Gaps		1.1052	116,903	-0.0903	-0.1802	-0.0229	-0.0474	0.9449	-0.0588	-0.1110	-0.0337	-0.0483	0.3631
Market Moving Down	1 Day	1.3638	26,569	-0.1482	-0.1531	-0.0677	-0.0002	0.8802	-0.1363	-0.2211	-0.1644	-0.1486	0.2592
	3 day	1.2623	26,983	-0.1398	-0.2936	-0.0076	-0.0838	0.6138	-0.0597	-0.1442	0.0163	-0.0152	0.2675
	5 Day	1.2358	33,065	-0.3379	-0.2842	-0.0317	-0.2049	0.5725	-0.1579	-0.1295	0.0156	-0.0148	0.1889
	10 Day	1.1632	39,568	-0.2186	-0.0983	-0.1382	-0.4352	0.6917	-0.1085	-0.1051	-0.0609	-0.1726	-0.0001
	30 Day	1.1753	39,883	-0.1968	-0.1591	-0.0236	-0.0442	0.9143	-0.1003	-0.1598	-0.0969	-0.2417	-0.2078
	90 Day	1.1884	43,931	-0.1562	-0.3087	-0.0221	-0.1891	0.7455	-0.0670	-0.1330	0.0024	-0.0149	0.4560
Market Moving Up	1 Day	1.0292	90,334	-0.0733	-0.1881	-0.0098	-0.0613	0.9639	-0.0360	-0.0787	0.0048	-0.0188	0.3937
	3 day	1.0581	89,920	-0.0755	-0.1462	-0.0275	-0.0365	1.0442	-0.0585	-0.1011	-0.0487	-0.0582	0.3918
	5 Day	1.0537	83,838	0.0073	-0.1392	-0.0195	0.0147	1.0918	-0.0197	-0.1038	-0.0531	-0.0615	0.4319
	10 Day	1.0756	77,335	-0.0247	-0.2221	0.0360	0.1510	1.0744	-0.0334	-0.1141	-0.0197	0.0153	0.5490
	30 Day	1.0689	77,020	-0.0352	-0.1911	-0.0226	-0.0491	0.9607	-0.0373	-0.0858	-0.0009	0.0519	0.6588
	90 Day	1.0551	72,972	-0.0506	-0.1028	-0.0234	0.0379	1.0649	-0.0539	-0.0978	-0.0554	-0.0684	0.3072

So what can you conclude from these two tables? For up gaps, prior market movements don't seem to impact returns (both unadjusted and market-adjusted) in any identifiable manner. The same is true for down gaps, but there is one interesting difference to consider. The returns for long positions are generally higher if the prior market movement is also down. However, there isn't much difference when the returns are market adjusted.

The market up/market down approach is simple but does not distinguish between low and high values; a return of +0.2% is counted as up, but so is a return of +20%. With the second approach, we put the return into one of five categories: market strongly up, market up, market steady, market down, or market strongly down. The groupings are akin to the volume groupings used in Chapter 6, but the procedure for determining the groupings was quite different. The same procedure was used for the 1-, 3-, 5-, 10-, 30-, and 60-day market returns, but we used the 1-day returns to describe the process. We took all the 1-day market returns for all 17 years in the study and sorted them from lowest to highest. Then we identified the bottom 10%, bottom 25%, top 25%, and top 10% of the returns. If the return was in the bottom 10%, we labeled it as "market strongly down." If it was in the bottom 25%, we labeled it as "market down." We designated the top returns similarly. All returns that fell in the middle were labeled as "market steady."

This approach does have some problems with it. Data is used in later periods to determine a value for something that occurred in an earlier period. An investor in 1995 would have had no way to know whether, for example, the 5-day market return that was just observed would have been a case that could be considered "market strongly down" relative to market returns over the 1995–2011 time period. Therefore, the analysis using this approach merits some caution.

Tables 8.7 and 8.8 show the results from this second approach. Again, focus on whether market movements should have a bearing on how you analyze gaps. Consider the extreme cases first. Focus on the "market strongly down" versus the "market strongly up" sections in Table 8.7. Do you see much of a difference? Yes and no. There are 60 data cells in the unadjusted and market-adjusted entries in the "market strongly up" section of the table. All but 4 of the 60 have positive values. If you look at the "market strongly down" section, there are 42 cells with positive values, about two-thirds of the values. So overall the results are somewhat similar. However, most of the negative values in the "market strongly down" section are in the upper-left corner of the two subsections ("Returns" and "Market-Adjusted Returns"). What does this tell you concerning an investment strategy?

You generally want to go long on a down gap expecting a reversal regardless of the prior market direction. But if the market has been strongly down over just the last 1, 3, 5, or 10 days, then the downward move of the stock may continue for the next 1 to 5 days.

Another difference between the two strong movement scenarios is that the returns are larger in 54 out of the 60 cells for the market strongly up section compared to the market strongly down section. So any reversal that may occur is probably going to be stronger if the market is up strongly.

TABLE 8.7　Returns for Down Gaps in Various Market Conditions

Down Gaps		Average Gap Size	Number of Occurences	Returns					Market-Adjusted Returns				
				1-day	3-day	5-day	10-day	30-day	1-day	3-day	5-day	10-day	30-day
Market Strongly Down	1 Day	-1.1095	20,580	-0.1699	-0.1356	0.0260	0.0585	1.0864	-0.1430	-0.0797	-0.1052	-0.1051	0.1902
	3 day	-1.1182	22,522	-0.2276	-0.1504	-0.0291	0.6179	1.6375	-0.0951	-0.0340	0.0383	0.3471	0.6320
	5 Day	-1.2112	20,278	-0.0422	0.2862	0.3251	1.3692	1.4215	-0.0288	0.0560	0.1001	0.5125	0.4099
	10 Day	-1.2300	18,203	-0.1734	-0.2568	0.0386	0.4444	1.9092	-0.1024	-0.1553	-0.1746	0.1719	0.7068
	30 Day	-1.2912	16,964	0.0355	0.3927	0.6496	0.7636	2.0135	0.0137	0.0221	0.0990	0.1976	0.6077
	90 Day	-1.3956	19,572	0.0864	0.2430	0.7580	0.8183	1.2176	0.0210	0.0857	0.0686	0.2233	0.5725
Market Down	1 Day	-1.1725	34,786	0.1755	0.2761	0.9362	1.1614	1.4250	-0.0778	0.0423	0.0918	0.1718	0.5120
	3 day	-1.2400	30,691	0.2511	0.2623	1.1629	1.1540	2.7109	-0.0603	0.0380	0.1464	0.1301	0.6150
	5 Day	-1.2505	24,470	0.1413	0.1786	1.0008	0.3690	3.5784	-0.0050	0.1343	0.1725	0.0002	1.1005
	10 Day	-1.3789	22,104	0.0456	0.0363	1.0201	1.2506	2.6008	-0.1173	0.0703	0.2247	0.3188	0.6071
	30 Day	-1.4602	19,350	-0.1522	-0.6135	0.5934	0.5686	1.6132	-0.2910	-0.2802	-0.0085	-0.0116	0.3374
	90 Day	-1.5099	19,159	0.1182	0.0336	0.6930	0.4616	2.1478	-0.1844	-0.0563	0.0450	0.0112	0.6526
Market Steady	1 Day	-1.4315	33,213	-0.1712	-0.2286	-0.0062	-0.0063	0.4174	-0.0064	-0.0713	0.0098	0.0586	0.1757
	3 day	-1.3893	35,099	-0.1098	-0.1266	0.0453	-0.1040	0.0338	-0.0327	-0.0546	-0.0426	-0.0832	-0.0836
	5 Day	-1.3477	40,523	-0.0820	-0.0205	0.2583	0.4074	0.3284	-0.0927	-0.0562	-0.0398	-0.0039	-0.1127
	10 Day	-1.3104	40,930	-0.0241	-0.0013	0.1539	-0.1230	0.4797	-0.0211	-0.0299	-0.0208	-0.1018	0.0493
	30 Day	-1.2788	44,191	-0.0398	0.0385	0.0015	0.2943	0.7295	-0.0187	0.0536	-0.0685	0.0420	0.1060
	90 Day	-1.2465	43,233	-0.1548	-0.1414	0.0396	0.1020	0.3633	-0.0505	-0.0158	0.0064	0.0302	-0.0717
Market Up	1 Day	-1.9786	5,634	0.0874	0.1398	0.2701	0.4920	1.6470	0.0834	0.1776	0.3656	0.5869	1.3075
	3 day	-1.8927	5,946	-0.1555	0.0357	-0.2866	-0.1319	0.2870	-0.0389	-0.0520	-0.1484	-0.0712	0.1017
	5 Day	-1.6086	7,712	-0.1169	-0.4159	-0.8018	-0.8682	-1.4174	-0.0653	-0.0614	-0.0947	-0.0669	-0.3157
	10 Day	-1.4853	9,487	-0.0948	0.0056	0.2952	0.6718	1.7693	-0.0088	0.0497	0.1653	0.1591	0.6482
	30 Day	-1.4087	10,452	0.0266	0.1837	0.4161	0.3729	1.2171	0.0098	0.1002	0.2375	0.0266	0.4281
	90 Day	-1.2902	8,437	-0.0448	0.0208	0.1122	0.2874	1.3457	-0.0390	-0.0825	-0.0023	0.0590	0.3151
Market Strongly Up	1 Day	-2.7166	2,816	0.2157	0.6799	0.5675	0.8300	0.6010	0.1672	0.5006	0.4347	0.6265	0.6324
	3 day	-2.4189	2,771	0.0795	0.5384	0.3954	0.5796	3.0949	0.1636	0.6138	0.5977	0.8528	2.1393
	5 Day	-1.9236	4,046	-0.0875	-1.0419	0.1607	-0.0257	3.1597	0.0108	-0.4439	0.1802	0.2735	2.0928
	10 Day	-1.4857	6,305	0.3262	0.9186	0.5820	1.4966	0.4588	0.0763	0.3011	0.3377	0.5251	0.3576
	30 Day	-1.4104	6,072	0.3045	0.5777	1.4987	2.2135	3.4943	0.1978	0.2473	0.6037	0.9175	1.7641
	90 Day	-1.3494	6,628	0.1717	0.3706	0.7914	2.2347	5.9613	0.1077	0.0986	0.3283	0.6703	2.0277

TABLE 8.8 Returns for Up Gaps in Various Market Conditions

Up Gaps		Average Gap Size	Number of Occurences	Returns					Market-Adjusted Returns				
				1-day	3-day	5-day	10-day	30-day	1-day	3-day	5-day	10-day	30-day
Market Strongly Down	1 Day	1.8271	2,998	-0.2121	-0.0745	-0.0812	0.2254	0.3157	-0.1974	-0.3929	-0.5230	-0.2559	0.1066
	3 day	1.7591	2,905	0.0151	-0.5929	-1.0099	-0.6385	0.0198	-0.0793	-0.7986	-1.0217	-1.0587	-0.1656
	5 Day	1.5157	4,753	-0.2092	-0.3801	-0.0610	-1.4078	0.1597	-0.1148	-0.1574	-0.1581	-0.3534	0.0266
	10 Day	1.3658	7,171	-0.3054	0.4088	0.6289	-0.0063	2.0786	-0.0498	0.0741	0.1168	0.0102	0.3425
	30 Day	1.2749	9,805	-0.0973	-0.4931	-0.5184	-1.0453	0.8411	-0.0260	0.1108	-0.0061	-0.3538	-0.3941
	90 Day	1.4014	11,808	-0.6994	-0.5041	-0.1043	-0.7917	2.5145	-0.2477	-0.0606	0.1241	-0.2554	1.2986
Market Down	1 Day	1.4336	8,356	-0.0790	-0.0634	0.1084	0.0076	1.0844	-0.0916	-0.1560	-0.0171	-0.0982	0.5293
	3 day	1.3797	7,574	0.0392	0.1174	0.7240	0.8356	1.1899	0.0033	-0.0144	0.2817	0.2795	0.4162
	5 Day	1.2326	11,246	-0.5181	-0.0040	-0.3546	-0.1476	0.1756	-0.1904	-0.2096	-0.1028	-0.0536	-0.0964
	10 Day	1.1327	12,804	-0.0921	-0.0833	-0.1914	-0.1642	0.7708	-0.0825	-0.0584	0.0826	0.0773	0.1092
	30 Day	1.1965	15,915	-0.4662	-0.1306	0.2270	0.2348	1.1557	-0.2520	-0.2770	-0.1625	-0.4084	-0.2549
	90 Day	1.1084	20,443	0.0526	-0.1118	-0.1163	-0.0802	0.0008	0.0153	-0.1656	-0.0897	0.0973	0.3334
Market Steady	1 Day	1.1175	46,548	-0.1407	-0.1568	-0.0769	-0.0725	0.7763	-0.1274	-0.1911	-0.1259	-0.1851	0.2029
	3 day	1.0557	53,401	-0.1171	-0.1871	-0.1216	-0.1707	0.4416	-0.0762	-0.1123	-0.0857	-0.0807	0.1309
	5 Day	1.0720	55,853	-0.0851	-0.1552	0.0628	0.0896	0.9899	-0.0671	-0.1214	-0.0134	0.0286	0.4644
	10 Day	1.0528	60,199	-0.1122	-0.1641	-0.2371	-0.1924	0.4937	-0.0712	-0.1227	-0.1382	-0.1787	0.1329
	30 Day	1.0500	59,646	-0.0753	-0.0681	-0.0913	-0.1000	0.5498	-0.0404	-0.0600	-0.0523	-0.0404	0.2910
	90 Day	1.0840	56,763	-0.0658	-0.1853	-0.0888	-0.0262	0.6056	-0.0734	-0.1152	-0.0915	-0.0939	0.1567
Market Up	1 Day	0.9399	24,740	-0.1652	-0.3482	-0.3064	0.0845	0.5573	-0.0984	-0.1767	-0.1304	-0.0299	0.2154
	3 day	1.0149	24,553	-0.1584	-0.2248	-0.2748	-0.5996	-0.3129	-0.1259	-0.1772	-0.2026	-0.4278	-0.2594
	5 Day	1.0141	21,211	0.0930	0.0661	0.0013	-0.2471	0.9279	0.0271	0.0023	-0.0352	-0.1866	0.1838
	10 Day	1.0985	20,920	-0.0078	-0.1123	0.4507	0.2284	1.4880	-0.0332	-0.0810	0.1797	0.0382	0.6079
	30 Day	1.0975	18,446	0.1007	-0.4479	0.2937	0.3655	1.4405	-0.0024	-0.1338	0.1434	0.3697	1.0774
	90 Day	0.9986	16,009	-0.0318	-0.1599	0.1304	0.0456	0.4121	-0.0386	-0.1652	0.0029	-0.0064	-0.1417
Market Strongly Up	1 Day	1.0647	34,261	0.0401	-0.1284	0.2282	-0.1459	1.4748	0.0832	0.0807	0.2003	0.1547	0.6694
	3 day	1.3362	28,470	-0.0265	-0.1658	0.2814	0.4855	2.9008	0.0172	-0.0072	0.2264	0.3557	1.3756
	5 Day	1.1222	23,840	-0.0401	-0.3125	-0.0811	0.1279	1.3740	-0.0425	-0.1318	-0.0223	-0.0420	0.5694
	10 Day	1.1733	15,809	-0.0172	-0.6771	0.0068	0.2158	1.5712	-0.0303	-0.2332	-0.0806	0.2059	1.1309
	30 Day	1.1299	13,091	0.0341	-0.1395	-0.0903	0.0148	1.8680	-0.0119	-0.1101	-0.0623	-0.0064	1.0040
	90 Day	1.0503	11,880	0.0732	0.0211	0.3269	0.5222	3.3484	0.0440	0.0255	0.1328	0.0688	1.1513

Comparing the market down to the market up sections, the picture is not as clear. The most striking thing to observe in comparing those sections is that the returns (but not the market-adjusted returns) are lower for the market down section in all but 2 of the 30 cells.

For up gaps the prior market conditions don't seem to matter too much. Doing the same types of comparisons in Table 8.7 that you did in Table 8.6, you can see there isn't a marked difference between returns when the prior market movement was up versus down. This was the same conclusion reached when analyzing Table 8.5.

So, concluding this section of the chapter, should market movements influence your individual stock gap-based trading decisions? For up gaps the answer is "no" based on the analysis of Tables 8.5 and 8.6. Down gaps are a bit more complicated. In general, returns are higher for long positions when the prior market movement has been down. Generally, you want to go long on a down gap expecting a reversal regardless of the prior market direction. But if the market has been strongly down over just the last 1, 3, 5, or 10 days, then the downward move of the stock may continue for the next 1 to 5 days.

Summary

This is the longest chapter and there has been much to digest. You began by looking at the 25 days with the highest number (553 or more) of gaps. All 25 have occurred since 2007 and 14 were in 2011. This is another way in which market volatility has been manifested. The underlying causes behind these high gap days was discussed; many were heavily influenced by events outside the United States.

From an investing perspective, you looked at high gap days to see if they gave you any clue about future market direction. For example, if a high number of stocks gapped up on a particular day, is that a signal that the market is headed up or headed down? It did not appear that high gap days dominated by gaps in a particular direction give reliable market timing signals.

You considered two other ideas to make use of the high gap day list. One idea is to look to the dominant group for guidance. For example, if many stocks gapped and 99% of them gapped up, do those stocks that gapped up represent some type of trading opportunity? For days with a high number of down gaps, the best idea seems to be to go short on the down-gapping stocks on the day after the gap, looking for a downward continuation. But, after Day 1 it appears that it would be better to be long, hoping for a reversal. After Day 1 it appeared that being long is a solid idea. The magnitude of the returns is quite high, which is certainly intriguing. The data suggest a similar approach to trading gap up stocks on a day with many up gaps. For Day 1 prices are likely to continue moving up; a continuation approach looks best. After Day 1 a reversal strategy looks better, but the evidence here was not as strong as it was for the down gaps.

A second way to use the high gap day list would be to focus on the small number of stocks moving opposite to the herd. The returns here seem to offer some nice potential. But given the small sample size you dug into the details to see what was causing this group to move in an opposite direction from the majority. What you saw is that some dramatic company-specific event was the cause. Although there appears to be some potential in focusing on this group of stocks, each case needs to be considered separately.

You also examined whether prior market movements should influence gap-based trades. For example, assume that the market has been in a strong uptrend and you are considering whether to go long or short with stocks that have gapped up. Do you go long, staying with the stock's upward movement and the market's upward movement, or do you perhaps look for a reversal? For up gaps, you found that prior market movements had little impact. For down gaps it does have some impact. Generally go long on a down gap expecting a reversal regardless of the prior market direction. But, if the market has been strongly down over just the last 1, 3, 5, or 10 days, the downward move of the stock may continue for the next 1 to 5 days.

Chapter 9

Closing the Gap

"The gap must be closed" is an often-heard saying among traders. This saying, however, seems to be based on lore rather than on hard evidence. The idea is that a gap creates a void in the price on a stock chart, and there is a natural tendency for market participants to want to "fill the gap" so that no visual void appears on the chart. Even those who claim that a gap must be closed differ widely in their interpretations. Some think that the gap will close quickly, within a few trading days; others talk about this occurring over a much longer time period, perhaps even years.

The criterion used throughout this book to define a gap is that one day's price action lies totally out of the range of the previous day's price action. Thus, for an up gap, the Day 0 low must be higher than the Day –1 high. For a down gap, the Day 0 high must be lower than the Day –1 low. In candlestick terms, the candles cannot overlap—not even the wicks of the candles. This chapter considers the closing of gaps.

What does it mean for a gap to close? Say a stock gaps up. For a gap up to close, the low of some subsequent day needs to be lower than the Day 0 high. Some gaps close quickly, whereas others may not close for very long periods of time.

Timing of Closing Gaps

As we considered how long it takes for a gap to close, some timing issues became critical, leading us to consider gaps from a shorter period of time than we had earlier in this book. Throughout this book, we considered gaps that occurred through December 2011. Looking at gaps that occurred late in the time horizon— in December 2011, for example—it is quite possible that some gaps would not close by the time of this writing but would close soon afterward. We knew that we needed to provide plenty of time after the gaps occurred to allow for closures.

We wanted to examine how long it takes for gaps to close. Many of the gaps that occurred in December 2011, for example, would not have been closed by the end of December 2011. We knew we needed to consider gaps that occurred long enough ago to allow more time for gaps to close. This, by itself, would encourage us to focus on an early period of our dataset, perhaps the earliest year of 1995. But, we wanted to stay as close to the end of 2011 as possible. As we have seen, the incidence of gaps has increased dramatically in recent years, suggesting that gapping behavior itself may be fundamentally changing. General market conditions also can have an influence on the closing of gaps. It is easier for down gaps to close than for up gaps to close when the market is trending up. Thus, looking at a fairly recent time period that was not too biased as far as an uptrend or a downtrend in the market, but which was far enough back to provide time for gaps to close, was essential.

As a compromise between the various considerations, we chose to look at gaps that occurred between January 1, 2010, and June 30, 2010. As shown in Figure 9.1, the market had several up and down moves over that time period, so it wasn't unduly biased toward the closing of gaps in a certain direction. We stopped our computations concerning whether or not the gap closed at the end of December 2011. This gave every gap in the period at least a year-and-a-half to close.

During the January through June 2010 time period, 1,702 unique stocks experienced at least one gap. For those stocks, 10,766 gaps that met the liquidity criteria occurred. Of these 10,766 gaps, 5,373 were up gaps and 5,393 were down gaps. For up gaps, the median time to close was 5 days. For the down gaps, the median time to close was 6 days. Therefore, it appears that about half of the time gaps will close in about a week (5 trading days).

Now look at the closing of up gaps a little more closely. Figure 9.2 shows the number of up gaps that closed within 25 days of gapping. About 22.6% of the up gaps close the day after the gap. Another 11% of the up gaps close on Day 2. Thus, over one-third of the up gaps close within 2 days. Over half (53.6%) of up gaps closed by Day 5. By Day 8, two-thirds of the up gaps closed.

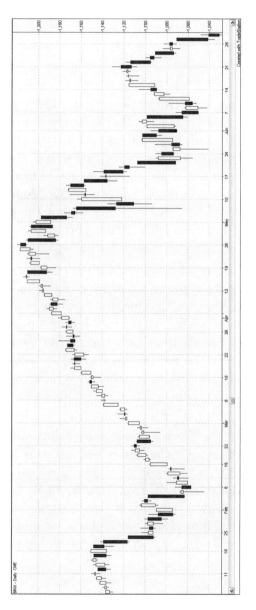

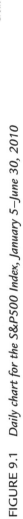

FIGURE 9.1   Daily chart for the S&P500 Index, January 5–June 30, 2010

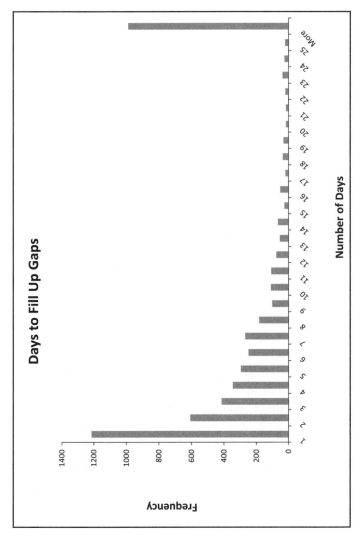

FIGURE 9.2 *Number of up gaps closed by days following gap*

After trading on Day 25, only 988 of the 5,373 up gaps, or 18%, had not been filled. As mentioned previously, December 30, 2011 was the cutoff date for the gaps to close. Every gap in the sample had at least one-and-a-half years to close before this cut-off date; gaps that occurred earlier in 2010 had even longer. By the end of 2011, 216 of the up gaps had still not closed. Thus, about 4% of the up gaps had not closed within at least 18 months. For example, the Crocs Inc. (CROX) up gap on January 4, 2010 at approximately $5 a share had still not closed by the end of 2011. The closing price at the end of the year was $14.77, which meant that it still needed to drop almost $9 more to close the gap that occurred almost 2 years before.

In Chapter 2, "Windows on Candlestick Charts," you considered some of the ways in which gaps were used by those practicing traditional Japanese candlestick charting. One of the rules of thumb followed by these practitioners is that if a gap is not closed within 3 days, the market probably has enough power to continue its trend for 13 more sessions. How does this mesh with what you see for the closing of up gaps in Figure 9.2? You do indeed see that many up gaps, more than 40%, close within 3 days. In the sample, 3,136 gaps remained unfilled after 3 days. Did these up gaps tend to have enough power for a trend in the direction of the gap to continue for 13 more trading days? We see that by Day 11 (8 days after the suggested 3-day observation period), 1,657 of the 3,136 gaps that remained on Day 3 had been filled. Over half of the gaps that had not been closed by Day 3 had been filled by Day 11. Because this is only 8 days after the suggested 3-day watch period, the idea that the unclosed up gap has the momentum to continue in an uptrend for 13 more sessions is not supported. [1]

You must also be careful not to conclude that because a gap has not closed that a trend in the direction of the gap is continuing. Look at the two up gaps shown for Hot Topic, Inc. (HOTT) in Figure 9.3. HOTT gapped up on April 13, 2011, and again the following day. The April 13 gap, labeled Gap A in the figure, did not close until 17 days later. The April 14 gap, labeled Gap B, closed 9 days after it occurred. Gap A is an example of a gap that did not close in 3 days and continued to be open for 13 more trading days. However, price was not trending upward in the direction of the gap; price was slowly falling to close the gap.

Now turn your attention to the closing of down gaps; information about these down gaps is provided in Figure 9.4. Almost 22% of down gaps close the following day. By Day 3, close to 36% of down gaps have closed. By Day 6, 55% of the down gaps have closed. Two-thirds of all the down gaps have closed by Day 11, and three-quarters have filled by Day 20.

Of the 5,393 down gaps, 1,191 remain open after 25 days of trading. Of these 1,191 gaps, 173 remained unclosed by the end of 2011. Thus, of all the down gaps, a little more than 3% remained unfilled over one-and-a-half years later. An example of an unfilled down gap would be the gap occurring for Monsanto (MON) on January 12, 2010 at $83 per share. At the end of 2011, almost 2 years later, MON was trading in the $72 range, and the gap remained unfilled.

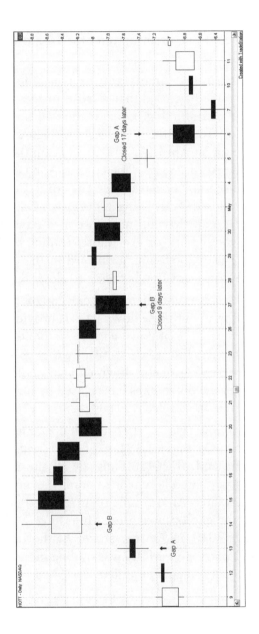

FIGURE 9.3   Daily stock chart for HOTT, April 9–May 11, 2011

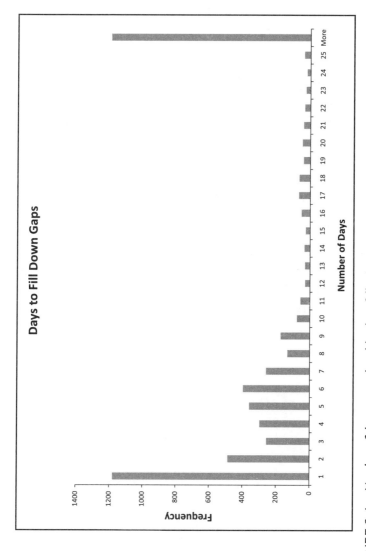

FIGURE 9.4 *Number of down gaps closed by days following gap*

What about the rule of thumb or waiting 3 days to see if a gap remains unfilled to confirm a trend in price? After the closing on Day 3, 3,472 gaps remained unfilled. By Day 11, 8 days later, more than half of those unfilled gaps were closed. Thus, if a gap remains at Day 3, chances are it will be closed by Day 11. Again, this evidence does not support the notion that the failure of a gap to close within 3 days suggests that a trend in the direction of the gap will continue for 13 more days.

Figure 9.5 shows an example of a gap that closed quickly. On February 23, 2011, Atmos Energy Corporation (ATO) gapped down, but the gap closed in 4 days, which is slightly faster than the median of 5 days.

For an example of a gap that is much slower to close, look at the February 28, 2010 gap for Jack in the Box (JACK) in Figure 9.6. This gap was not filled until June 24, 83 trading day later.

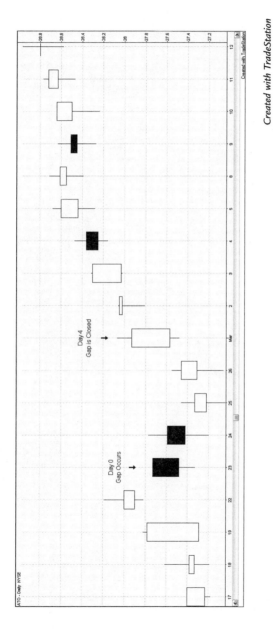

FIGURE 9.5   *Daily stock chart for ATO, February 17–March 12, 2010*

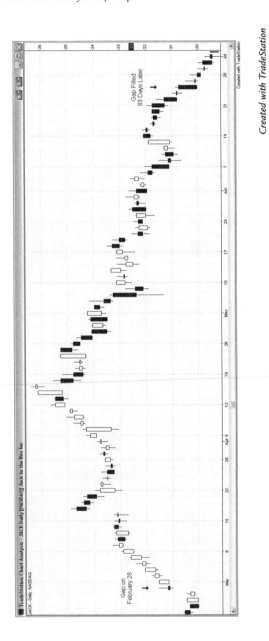

Created with TradeStation

FIGURE 9.6   *Daily stock chart for JACK, February 22– July 2, 2010*

Concluding Comments about Closing the Gap

As we have talked to a number of traders, the most frequent question about gaps is, "Doesn't a gap always close?" Based on the calculations, it appears that gaps may tend to close in roughly one trading week (5 days). For the sample of 10,766 gaps during the period January 1 to June 30, 2010, the median time to close for up gaps was 5 days, whereas the median time for down gaps to close was 6 days. Some of the gaps observed had still not closed more than 1 $1/_2$ years later.

Throughout this book, gaps have been discussed using daily bars. Sometimes a stock opens above the previous day's high or opens below the previous day's low, but subsequent price movement during the day causes the stock to not meet the criteria for a gap. This price behavior creates a gap on intraday charts but not on daily bar charts. Often, this is referred to as an "opening gap" because it creates a gap at the opening of the trading day, but it is filled within the day.

We have not done an exhaustive study of opening gaps. Because we have received so many questions regarding these gaps, we thought it would be helpful to mention something about the frequency of their occurrence. Of the 1,702 stocks considered in this chapter that did gap during the January–June 2010 time frame, 52,616 opening gaps occurred. Of these, 12,746 were not filled during the day. So approximately 76% of the opening gaps closed on the day they occurred, and about 24% became actual gaps. However, not all those 12,746 met the liquidity criteria; 10,779 of these gaps did meet the liquidity criteria and were included in the results in previous chapters.

Although this chapter presents some interesting information about price behavior around gaps, it hasn't led to any particular trading recommendations. A detailed study of this topic might lead to some intriguing trading possibilities, but it's also something that is not easily done. We may explore it in the future.

Endnotes

1. An important note is that the Japanese candlestick tradition is based on the notion that a "window is closed" rather than the author's idea of a gap closing. As explained in Chapter 2, in the Japanese tradition a window is closed only if the real body of a candle closes past the window. For the authors' analysis, if price fills the void intraday, the gap is considered closed. Therefore, a broader definition is used for the closing of a gap and a gap is considered closed when a Japanese candlestick analyst would still consider the window opened.

Chapter 10

Putting It All Together

D iscussions of gaps are frequent in the technical analysis literature. Pick up an issue of *Technical Analysis of Stocks and Commodities* or *Active Trader* and often there is an article that mentions gaps. Turn on the financial news, and you will probably not have to listen long before you hear gaps mentioned. Pick up a book on technical analysis, and you can find a discussion of gaps. Do an Internet search about technical analysis, and you can find a proliferation of Web sites that discuss gaps. Although this interest in gaps is not new, there has been surprisingly little systematic study of gaps.

Technical analysis has traditionally been a visual activity. Although computer technology has allowed for algorithmically generated trading based on the techniques of technical analysis without a human looking at a chart, the technology has also allowed for more colorful and visually rich charting to reach the eyes of more and more traders. No longer does a trader need to construct charts by hand, nor does a trader have to wait for yesterday's data to begin constructing charts. Data and charts are available instantaneously. Although this has allowed for the quick recognition of more and more complicated patterns by a greater number of traders, the interest in basic tools such as gap analysis remains.

When we started systematically analyzing gaps, a few traders said that gaps were becoming an outdated tool. Their analysis was that gaps were becoming less and less frequent. Just as the move to decimalization caused the statistics for the number of stocks that were unchanged for a day to decrease, they reasoned that gaps would become less frequent. With price changes tracked at smaller increments, they reasoned, gaps would be less likely. They also cited increased market activity as a reason to postulate that gaps were becoming less frequent in the market. Thinly traded stocks tend to gap at a high rate because of discrete market activity. Thus, they reasoned, as more and more traders have instantaneous access to news and market information and trading volume increases, gaps will become less frequent. Thus, they would conclude, gaps are an interesting historical phenomenon in the markets, but they are becoming less and less useful to traders.

Surprisingly, we have found that this is not the case. In fact, we have found an increasing number of gaps in the past few years. And these gaps are not limited to small, lower volume companies. A number of gaps exist for high market cap stocks, such as AAPL, WMT, and MCD. In 2011, we found more than 32,000 instances of gaps; this was more than twice the number of gaps 5 years earlier and more than three times the number of gaps a decade earlier. Thus, a trader will not find a lack of gaps.

Two frequently heard phrases when analysts talk about gaps are "A gap is always filled" and "Trade in the direction of the gap." Interestingly, these two bits of advice are somewhat at odds with each other. Suppose a stock gaps up. A filling of the gap would mean a price reversal occurs as price falls to close the gap. If this occurs, a short position would be profitable. If, instead, the price movement is going to continue in the direction of the gap, price will rise and a long position would be profitable.

One way this conflicting advice could be resolved is that a gap is quickly filled, somewhat in a price rebound, and then price continues in the direction of the gap. To see if this happens, this book considers price movement in the short term, 1, 3, and 5 days after a gap and then a bit longer, 10 and 30 days after a gap. The general results, presented in Chapter 2, "Windows on Candlestick Charts," point to an immediate price reversal for up gaps. On average, when a stock gaps up, the price movement over the next 10 days tends to be in a negative direction. These results are consistent with what you can find in Chapter 9, "Closing the Gap," when the average up gap is closed within 5 days. However, by 30 days, the upward movement in the direction of the gap has, on average, returned.

What about down gaps? Chapter 2 discusses that the negative price movement tends to continue the day after a down gap. However, by Day 3 the price trends upward. Stocks that experience down gaps have, on average, positive 3-, 5-, 10-, and 30-day returns. These results are consistent with what you learned in Chapter 9 about the filling of down gaps. The average down gap is filled within 6 trading days.

Of course, looking at averages over a large sample size can mask some underlying tendencies of some particular groups of stocks. Chapters 5, 6, and 7 examine the impact of other variables.

Chapter 5, "Gaps and Previous Price Movement," examines the impact of price movement on Day 0 (day of the gap) and Day –1. In candlestick terms, you studied the importance of white versus black candles on those 2 days.

You might think that spotting a black candle followed by another black candle that gaps down would be an ominous sign that downward price movement is gaining momentum. However, the results show that when a black candle on Day –1 is followed by a gap on Day 0, price movement tends to reverse to an upward direction on Day 1, and this upward movement continues for at least 30 days. This suggests that the downward gap was an overreaction and the price fell too far. Likewise, you might think that an up gap, especially when it occurs in a White-Up-White pattern, suggests strong upward price momentum. Again, the results bring this traditional reasoning into question. Stocks tend to reverse direction and have negative returns for a couple of weeks following an up gap.

Chapter 6, "Gaps and Volume," considers a classic variable used by technical analysts to confirm price movements: volume. Traditional analysis suggests that price movements, especially upward movements, on high volume are more meaningful than when they occur on low volume. However, the analysis of volume, as it relates to gaps, does not provide a great deal of useful information or added value. You saw in earlier chapters that gap downs tend to be followed by continued price decline on Day 1, but the price quickly shows reversal. The biggest insight that volume gives you is that price reversal tends to occur sooner for down gaps that occur on moderately low volume compared to those occurring on high volume. For example, low-volume down gaps tend to reverse on Day 1, whereas high volume down gaps tend not to reverse until after Day 3.

Chapter 7, "Relative Price of Gap Occurrence," focuses on the impact the price at which a gap occurs relative to the average price for the stock has on the profitability of trading strategies. Most up gaps occur at above average prices and most down gaps occur at below average prices. The vast majority of gaps occur within a 75% to 125% range of the stock's price moving average. Some gaps, however, do occur at extremely high or extremely low price levels. A consistent result is that stocks that gap down at above average prices tend to reverse price direction immediately. This suggests that purchasing a stock that gaps down on Day 0 at an above average price at the opening the following day, Day 1, can, on average, be a profitable trading strategy.

Stocks that gap up tend to have negative returns immediately following the gap. These negative returns tend to occur for a longer period of time for the stocks that gap up at relatively low prices. Stocks that gap up at a price below their 10-day, 30-day, or 90-day moving average still have negative returns at the 10-day holding period. By the 30-day mark, these returns have become positive.

The first part of Chapter 8, "Gaps and the Market," studied the 25 days (from 1995–2011) with the highest number (553 or more) of gaps. All 25 have occurred since 2007 and 14 were in 2011. Investors know that 2011 was extremely volatile. The high gap activity was another way in which market volatility was manifested. Also discussed are the underlying causes behind these high gap days. Many were heavily influenced by events outside the United States.

From an investing perspective, you looked at high gap days to see if they gave any clue about future market direction. For example, if a high number of stocks gapped up on a particular day, is that a signal that the market is headed up or headed down? It did not appear that high gap days dominated by gaps in a particular direction give reliable market timing signals.

Two other ideas were considered for making use of the high gap day list. One idea is to look to the dominant group for guidance. For example, if many stocks gapped and 99% of them gapped up, do those stocks that gapped up represent some type of trading opportunity? For days with a high number of down gaps, the best idea seems to be to go short on the down-gapping stocks on the day after the gap, looking for a downward continuation. But, after Day 1 it appears that it would be better to be long, hoping for a reversal. After Day 1 it appears that being long is a solid idea. The magnitude of the returns is quite high, which is certainly intriguing. The data suggest a similar approach to trading gap up stocks on a day with many up gaps. For Day 1 prices are likely to continue moving up; a continuation approach looks best. After Day 1 a reversal strategy looks better, but the evidence here was not as strong as it was for the down gaps.

A second way to use the high gap day list would be to focus on the small number of stocks moving opposite to the herd. The returns here seem to offer some nice potential. But given the small sample size, you dug into the details to see what was causing this group to move in an opposite direction from the majority. What you saw is that some dramatic company-specific event was the cause. Although there appears to be some potential in focusing on this group of stocks, each case needs to be considered separately.

You also examined whether prior market movements should influence your gap-based trades. For example, assume that the market has been in a strong uptrend and you are considering whether to go long or short with stocks that have gapped up. Do you go long, staying with the stock's upward movement and the market's upward movement, or do you perhaps look for a reversal? For up gaps, prior market movements had little impact. For down gaps it does have some impact. Generally you want to go long on a down gap expecting a reversal regardless of the prior market direction. But, if the market has been strongly down over just the last 1, 3, 5, or 10 days, then the downward move of the stock may continue for the next 1 to 5 days.

It would be nice to say that we found the Holy Grail vis-à-vis gap trading, but we have not. However, we think that this book provided some useful information to help guide gap-based trading. We thought that the consideration of some variables, such as volume, might greatly improve results, but were disappointed to find the variable studied didn't have more impact on returns. However, that a particular variable doesn't provide much help is, in itself, useful. Consider an analogy. Suppose you are about to start searching for diamonds in a square 4-acre field. If someone says, "I've looked hard in the northwest, northeast, and southeast quadrants and haven't found anything," is that valuable information? It is, assuming you trust the person who is making the statement.

For now, gaps seem to be here to stay. If the recent trend continues, you may see even more gaps. In the search for higher returns, this book provided some good clues of where to focus your efforts and some guidance concerning things that are probably a waste of time. The authors began this book planning to produce an in-depth study that would say most everything that could be said about gaps. However, gaps have proved to be even more interesting than imagined. Stay tuned. The study of gaps will probably continue. At least, after we take a short break.

I N D E X

Symbols

FINANCIAL TIMES

In an increasingly competitive world, it is quality of thinking that gives an edge—an idea that opens new doors, a technique that solves a problem, or an insight that simply helps make sense of it all.

We work with leading authors in the various arenas of business and finance to bring cutting-edge thinking and best-learning practices to a global market.

It is our goal to create world-class print publications and electronic products that give readers knowledge and understanding that can then be applied, whether studying or at work.

To find out more about our business products, you can visit us at www.ftpress.com.